# Reflections

## Edited by Lynn Picknett & Jason Roach

GOLD DUST
PUBLISHING
★ ★ ★

Reflections

e-book ISBN-13: 979-8-9868862-5-1
Paperback ISBN-13: 979-8-9868862-6-8


Cover design by: S. H. Roddey
Edited by Lynn Picknett & Jason Roach
Printed in the United States of America

"All young people, regardless of sexual orientation or identity, deserve a safe and supportive environment in which to achieve their full potential."

- Harvey Milk

To those who have lost their lives so that we could have progress. Also, To those who are suffering, those who are in need, and those whose rights are being taken away, we see you, we hear you, and we stand with you! But most of all, we love you.

# CONTENTS

# FOREWORD

How many times has someone said, "If I could go back and tell myself what I know now…" I know I've said it a few times over the years. Before I got married, I came across a ton of pictures of myself while looking for my birth certificate. They ranged from my early childhood into young adulthood. I found myself getting emotional as the memories flowed through my mind. Some were great. Some I didn't care to relive. Afterward, I made a social media post that went something like this:

1. Don't be afraid to be yourself.
2. Don't listen to those who make fun of you for being different. Many of them will come back years later and apologize.
3. Build lasting friendships and not enemies. Life's too short.
4. Death will influence you from many different angles. Don't let it harden you, but you may have already let that happen.

5. Don't take what's not yours, even if it's willing to give itself.
6. It's ok. One day, you're going to be a college graduate with three degrees, maybe four.
7. You're not fat.
8. You will have friends that love you. Cherish them and the time you have with them.
9. It's perfectly ok to cry.
10. Despite differences, your family loves you in their own way.

Each of these are great points to reflect on. I'm sure most of you have even told yourself some of these exact things. The crazy thing about this is looking at each one of these two years later, they have different meanings. It's crazy how time and life can make a difference. I wonder if at any time the authors who have written these letters will have the same experience.

I'd like to take a little time to make a few additions to these. The first that stands out is "Build lasting friendships and not enemies. Life's too short." This is great advice. But it becomes even more surreal after being diagnosed with bladder cancer at the end of 2022. And while everything is okay for now, it didn't help the fact that I found myself for the better part of 2023 in a deep dark place of depression. Not able to do the things I loved. No motivation to keep going. It was as if the cancer had already taken me away. It'd definitely caused me to lose the person I once knew. Everything had to change. The most important one was to stop smoking. It was not something I wanted to do.

There are quite a few amendments to this one. The most important would be to tell the boy in those pictures that the demons you fought in your early to mid-twenties will return twenty years later. Keep fighting them and don't let them win. You still have things to accomplish. The next thing I would say is that while it's important to not make enemies, it's completely okay to cut people out of your life, especially the vampires who suck the life out of you or those who marinate in negativity. On the flipside empathy and compassion are also traits that you could do well with. It will be hard at times, taking longer than others for those things sink in, but it will happen. Life's too short to dwell on the past and things that cannot be changed but focus on those lasting friendships. That's what's important. That's where you will find solace.

On top of that, I would tell him how it's also okay to say "No!" You don't have to be a people pleaser. Those constantly giving you guilt trips because you don't do every little thing they want you to do when they want you to do it and how they want you to do it are not the ones who get to dictate your life. You control your life and what amounts you give and take of it. This would also be a great addition to "Don't take what's not yours…" and don't give what's not theirs.

While I ended up completing three degrees, what I didn't know at the time of creating the post was that I would become a published author who got the chance to work with my favorite author as an editor. At this time in 2021, I hadn't even started my first book. I didn't know I would love that process so much that I'd open my own indie publishing company for LGBTQIA+ authors and allies. I didn't know that my husband would open a nonprofit and here I would be – compiling a book of letters to help fund his dreams for the LGBTQIA+ community. I didn't know that I would be surrounded by a group of supportive people in my newly chosen industry. I think back to the things I wrote in high school and in the early 2000s. I would most definitely tell that kid to follow those passions. Could you have imagined what it would have been worth had we (me) done that back then? I'd also tell him getting that passion back is going to be a lot of hard work, but it's going to be worth it.

In the end, the things I would go back and tell myself all circle back around to the very first one on the list. Don't be afraid to be yourself. Don't be afraid to stand up for yourself. Don't be afraid to take care of yourself, as you are unique, and there is only one of you. Stop letting people tell you how you should behave, and what emotions you should have. It is okay to not conform to what people tell you are gender norms. Persecution will come in many different forms and from all different angles of life. No this is not referring to what some would say as "being rebellious." Don't let it get the best of you. Don't let it change you, because it will try.

I used to tell myself and others that if I could go back, I wouldn't change a thing. But that's a lie. There's a lot I would change by taking a lot of this advice to heart. Granted if things hadn't gone the way they did throughout the years, I wouldn't be the person I am today. I wouldn't have the wonderfully supportive husband I have today. But I also think about how much better of a person I could have been had I not let things like death, bigotry, hatred, fear, religion, and other people control my life at times. I was asked the other day about what I thought contributed to LGBTQIA+ culture. While I couldn't speak for everyone else, those things were my culture. It was all I knew. Those were the things that made up my life Those were the demons I was constantly trying to escape.

During the creative process of this collection, I heard from many of the authors that this process was therapeutic or that they learned something about themselves. Even writing this forward, I can see where getting some of these things down on paper provides a sense of relief. I hope that this is the case with each of you, the readers. As you venture through the vulnerability of these pages, may these letters speak to you. May they help you heal from life's past traumas or encourage you to reflect on yourself and then move forward.

Some of these letters are not for the light of heart and dig deep into some of the author's personal fears, traumas, and persecutions. They fight many forms of abuse, loss, religious traumas, life changes, inner hatred and outer hatred. Others are lighthearted with fun little quips that will hopefully bring a smile to your face. Most importantly, all of them are encouraging, empowering, and inspiring. I wish you the best on this journey as we reflect and learn from our past. I challenge you to reflect on yourself as you move through each of these letters. You may find yourself in them.

Jason Roach
Author of The House on Dead Man's Curve
Editor in Chief – Gold Dust Publishing, LLC

# LONGING TO BE SEEN

You told me, "To thine own self be true,"
But what you meant was I should be like you.
Now that you find
we are not of one mind
You seem hurt but I'm hurting too.

You told me to value others' lives,
To respect them though theirs are not like mine,
But I deserve that too,
Don't dismiss me like you do.
I am more than what you define.

I am the ocean beneath a rising moon.
I am the sun that is setting too soon.
I am the summer wind stirring in the trees.
I am a rainbow longing to be seen.

Can you ask the sea to silence?
The sun forbear to shine?
Can you conceal a rainbow?
Can you stop the sands of time?

I am a part of you
But I have to be me.
You are a part of me,
Just love me
And let me be seen.

Sherry Blevins
Music composer

# DEAR SEAN,

As you graduate high school today, know that before you is the long road of adulthood. The on-ramp that is college may last as long as 4 years but be prepared for a few potholes and bumps along the way. Even if these become detours, keep your eyes focused on the horizon and the life you want to live, not the disappointments of the one you are living now.

You are a talented writer, but just like any other muscle, its development requires practice and hard work. Don't be lazy with either. You have stories to tell. What's more, you have stories that other people want to read. Write everything down, no matter how minor. True connection comes from relating to the world around you. As in life, your writing should not attempt to escape the world around you, but rather embrace it.

Kindness is not weakness. Act in a way that would make you proud to be the man you see in the mirror every day. Treat the people around you not only as you would want to be treated, but in a way that makes their day better. Be the change you want to experience.

You have losses ahead of you, these are unavoidable. Fortunately, these losses will be mixed with triumphs. After each heartbreak, you will find the sweetness of friendship and the support of those who love you. Take time to appreciate those close to you. They won't last forever, but you will carry the time you spend with them in your heart forever.

Enjoy your life, for good and ill. You only have one trip through this crazy world, make the most of it.

Sincerely,

Sean Harby
Author

# TO MY SIX-YEAR-OLD SELF,

This is the year you got sick with pneumonia and scarlet fever at the same time. This is the time that you recognized a shift in how you experience the world. You spent a lot of time trying to manage a chaotic environment, turning you into the world's worst people pleaser and obsessively hypervigilant to the energy around you. The problem was you didn't know it was energy, so you snapped into survival mode and just stayed there for thirty-four years. This manifests into all kinds of other issues for you like massive anxiety, OCD, and later physically as endometriosis, adenomyosis, and acute appendicitis, all at the same time. I wanted to write you this letter to let you know that you are going to be okay, so take a deep breath and close your eyes.

One day, your sensitivity will be your superpower. It will help you help others find themselves and their own spiritual path. You will become a powerful channel of source energy, a powerful healer. People will come to you not knowing why but knowing that they need something that your light has to offer. People will stop telling you that you are too sensitive with a negative connotation. People will flock to your light.

One day, you will no longer feel the need to manage the emotions of others to feel safe. Just because your parents couldn't emotionally regulate, doesn't mean you won't learn to, because you absolutely will. You will fall in love hard three times in life to help you with this process. The first time will absolutely destroy your soul and it will take you sixteen years to pick up the pieces. The second time is with a human who wants to help fix you because he sees what's underneath the rubble of destruction laid waste after the first marriage ended. He will become your biggest supporter and ally, long after the romantic relationship ends. The third time will be with someone who loves you, flaws and all. He will fight for you to become the best version of yourself. He will let you walk the journey alone, but his hand will never be far away when and if you need it. He will love every iteration of you, regardless of the amount of change. He supports your crazy new paranormal/ healer life because he knew how miserable you had been prior to starting that journey. He will be the one who says, "I just want you to be happy," and mean it. He is your soul's other half.

One day, you will stop working yourself to death as your way to find worth in others' eyes. You will find a tribe of people who fiercely love you for you. Not what you can offer them but because your soul lights them up too. These people will scoop you up, take you along for a ride you were never prepared for, and make sure you navigate it relatively unscathed. They will want to put you on display for all the right reasons. They seem to have an innate ability to understand the gift that you are, even before you do. You will learn the difficult things are what made you strong. The difficult things are also the things that keep you soft around the edges. The ability to sharply be able to discern what someone is going through, without them ever having to speak a word, helps you handle humans with care.

One day, you will stand up tall and say "I love me. I am proud that I have survived this far. If you don't love me for who I am in this exact moment, then there is no need for you to be in my life." You will finally learn to set boundaries: although sticking to them can still be hard, you understand their necessity and keep trying.

One day, you will suffer heart-crushing blows through the loss of humans and dogs to death. But worse than that, people will leave you because they can't handle your light, or that you are finally in your winning season. But that's okay too, because along the way, you have found that incredible tribe of people willing to pick you up and carry you when it all falls apart.

One day, you will learn that being in control all the time is a survival tactic. You have finally learned to flip on your back, float, and let the universe carry you to the next thing meant for you. You will never have to doubt the universe and your controlling ways just sort of disappear, except when driving. You will always want to be behind the wheel and that's ok.

One day, you will stop caring that you gave up a lucrative, stress-filled career in law. You don't care what's next, because you are finally living your authentic life and won't settle for anything less than what lights you up. You learn that happiness isn't money or satisfying the expectations of others. Happiness is in moments. Some we create, some we witness. You learn the power is in recognizing those moments as they are happening. You learn that you can't do that by living in fear. So you stop living in fear and start saying yes to all kinds of opportunities.

One day, you will learn that you were perfect at six. Just like you are now perfect at forty-four. And perfect means loving yourself, flaws and all. It means loving yourself regardless of what others have to say about you and your life. You will stop apologizing for taking up space in your own life, learning that the shadows of life you faced are the parts that helped ensure survival. You may not like them but will learn to love them and the role they played. You will make better choices in all aspects of your life.

One day, you will be asked to write this letter and maybe your story will become someone else's survival guide. And on this day, you celebrate being alive, celebrate living a life YOU created. The life you live is now filled with mystery, intrigue, energy work, ghostly adventures, graphic design, podcast appearances, fun admin work, travel, and the most amazing humans. You celebrate eight years of sobriety next week.

You will be writing this letter with tears of gratitude streaming down your face because this life was created by finally deciding to put yourself first. Once that decision was made, the universe just opened all the doors and kicked you right through them. You just got back from an eighteen-day working trip to one of the most haunted locations in the country. You had a blast, got dirty, sweaty, sunburned, and spent time with dear friends who helped you learn the ropes while embracing you as one of their own. It was the adventure of a lifetime, and you get to do it again. As often as you want, when schedules allow.

You will finally learn the balance of helping others purely for the sake of helping them, not because you need external validation. As a result, the opportunities just keep pouring in. Your vibration finally aligns with the soul at its core, and the universe matches it. Enjoy this time. It may come to a screeching halt one day. You will always maintain a perspective of wonder at how you got here, but nothing outweighs the gratitude you have for it all.

Keep learning, growing, and being nice to others. Keep smiling and complimenting strangers. Stay wild, moon child. The universe has bigger plans for you. I love you, I see you, and I honor you.

Love,

Erin

# DEAR YOUNGER SELF,

Stop rolling your eyes and muttering to yourself. Leave your hands where I can see them. Yes, I know you (I *am* you) and how you (I) respond to this kind of talk. These are just some things you (I) need to read (write) and some things I wish we had known ages ago. Life isn't as long as you think it is. Some of your therapists have been asking you to do this for a while. Why are we so stubborn?

Let's start there. Listen to (some of) your therapists and don't be afraid to ask for that help. There is no shame in needing and seeking it out. If that help comes in the form of medication because there are some things beyond your control, that does not mean something is *wrong* with you and that you can't beat something beatable or simple. That shame, embarrassment, and doubt are going to do more harm than good: try to let that go.

In asking for help, you may end up sharing more about yourself than you thought you could or would. Lean into that. It will seem scary at first and there will be a lot of questions; however, the sooner you share this, the sooner you'll learn how much you are loved and supported. That love and support will take active form sooner rather than later and you won't have to endure as much as you have already endured. This turns you into someone you don't always love being. You don't want to be that hard person. Talk sooner, ask for help sooner, and trust your people sooner.

You're snarky, that's fine, it can be fun, but don't let it cloud how you see people, how you see the world, and how people perceive you. It's okay to smile; it's okay to walk without focusing on *how* you look while doing it; it's okay to use your actual voice. Your face will freeze into an I-don't-give-a-fuck-about-you-or-anyone-or-the-world scowl and that's not the real you. Your voice will stay in a devil-may-care monotone that will be hard to break from and that's not the real you, either. Don't allow people to permanently alter who you are, how you see the world, and what you put out into the world.

It's okay to be opinionated; it's even okay to state those opinions in strident tones; however, don't condescend. Don't be an asshole. Your opinion isn't the only one that matters and trying to change people's minds about subjective things like art and music isn't pretty. Don't do it.

Believe people when they tell you you're loved, you're enough, you're talented or special. Hell, even believe them when they tell you you're great! The more time you spend doubting all of it, the more time you spend retreating into a place that becomes harder and harder to crawl out of, and by the time you do crawl out, you may think it's too late (or it may even be too late for some things that life has to offer). Have more faith in yourself, in what you do, and who you are.

Not everyone will like you; do not pander. That kind of desperation and wanting is exhausting. You don't like everybody, so what sense does it make for everyone to like you? Don't take out on the world what has happened to you. It's not *everyone's* fault, so don't treat everyone like the enemy, and don't compromise yourself for those same people you question. Authenticity is going to be very important to you. Start now.

Read more. Watch more. Listen more. You will end up respecting and admiring many things in what you read, watch, and listen to; look ahead with those things in mind. Mirror that. There is so much to enjoy and love about your life, hold onto those things and aim for more of those moments. I'm sorry you missed out on so many things. I'm sorry I prevented you from seeking help sooner. I'm sorry you were "born too soon and started too late" (you'll learn to *really* admire Sondheim, trust me). Don't let bitterness strangle you. Yes, things could have been easier, and different choices could have been made, altering your trajectory entirely; however, what you have now is great. Remember that, hold onto that, look ahead with all you've learned, and be kind to yourself and to other people. Tell your father you love him.

Vincent DiGeronimo
Musician, songwriter

# DEAR NICOLE (AT 16),

Hi. It's me, well, you. I'm an older version of you, but still the little weird girl from the housing projects caught between worlds. I wish I could tell you we grew out of being awkward and strange.

We didn't.

Wait! There's good news!

We—you—us discover others who are also awkward and strange. Our shameful feelings of being different, of confusion about who you crush on, about what you love, all of those painful daggers to your identity, will leave lasting scars; however, you will find your true family, your place of belonging, and friends who will draw stars around those scars.

I can't give you specifics about our future without ripping the space-time continuum. But I can give you some truths to ease the inner struggle you're wrestling with right now.

Here are a few things I wished I'd known when we were sixteen.

- Your Blackness is beautiful despite what the media tells you.
- Your weirdness is a blessing, lean into it.
- Your queerness is *normal*. You're not an anomaly or bound for Hell.
- You are worth loving-just as you are—quirky, smart, nerd, geek, bisexual self.
- The people who mock and hurt you, who tease and taunt you, hate themselves. They're pushing those negative feelings onto you. Be a duck, let it roll off.
- Band is amazing. Stick with it.
- Depression is real! The suicide attempt isn't a call for attention. Go see the counselor. Talk to every adult until you find someone who takes you and your mental health seriously.
- Listen to your inner voice. You doubt it all the time, but it is *right. Every. Time.*
- *No* is a complete sentence. Use it often to craft boundaries to protect themselves.
- Risk being disliked. Popularity in high school fades once you graduate, but the experiences and scars from betraying yourself do not.
- The man who promises you the world is a liar. Run. Away. *Fast.*

With the long, clear vision of hindsight, I share these words of wisdom with you. Write them down in our journal. Make them the guide for how we move through the world. It will spare you some heartache. Not all of it but we can all benefit from moving through life with a little less emotional trauma and baggage. Put it down. It's heavy.

I love us—you—me. Always.

Sincerely,
Nicole [at 49]
Nicole Givens Kurtz
Author, Publisher & Owner Mocha Memoirs Press

# NOTE TO SELF

You are a child at heart, pure and innocent, so easily wounded, some will say far "too sensitive". Don't believe a word of it. You will remain as you were born, sweet and gentle, a free spirit. The time will come when you no longer feel ashamed of or burdened by your innate sentimentality. No longer will you perceive it as a weakness. In fact, your raw personal courage and stoic emotional strength will emerge unscathed by aspersions cast, some unwarranted scrutiny, and harsh judgments made by those ignorant of the relevance of your presence on Earth at this pivotal time in human evolution. Be impervious to criticism as you go forth. It will have benefits impossible to foresee. Gradually you will comprehend your worth, resulting in an unexpected role to play on the stage of life. Prepare yourself. Rise to the occasion, as the forthcoming Paradigm Shift will occur during your lifetime.

Intuition is your saving grace. Trust it. Self-reflection holds the key to your ultimate liberation. It keeps you humbly grounded as you achieve milestones along a path less traveled. Once you have identified your purpose all will be revealed, illuminating the journey ahead. You shall begin dispersing the messages you've received, and they will travel around the world to those who are willing to listen. Be brave. Be fearless. Rise up against injustice. Your righteous indignation is not misplaced and will be defined by your observant nature as you watch this foreign world spinning around you. Allow yourself to be offended by it. Get angry whenever justifiable. Suffer grief with grace. In so doing, you will express yourself fully and live into your destiny. Find yourself. It will not only inform but will utterly transform your life experience as you become a formidable force to be reckoned with over time. When you consistently lift your voice up to the Universe, eventually others hear the call. Find your own kind. A sense of belonging will follow.

Yes, you are different, a weirdo by some accounts. Do not let the naysayers silence your song. Be the change you wish to see in the world. Be the Light you seek. Be a beacon in the night. Take it all in. Absorb then process all pertinent information that comes your way. Knowledge is power. Assess it. Dissect it. Study it. Be prepared to change your facile mind about it. Intellectual flexibility will prove to be essential to your own spiritual growth. With age comes wisdom.

No matter the many challenges and obstacles you will encounter, remain inherently optimistic. Don't allow yourself to get discouraged or caught in the trap of a societal expectation. You weren't born to fit in, you were born to kick down the sides of the flimsy cardboard box, not fit snuggly inside it. The many cats you will rescue over the course of your life will happily reside in the box you'll vacate as you outgrow it. Concepts of reality will be suddenly and irrevocably altered by what you witness in your youth. Decades later, these experiences will be painstakingly chronicled. The singular endeavor, a commitment to telling your tale will change countless lives and touch many hearts and minds.

You will look back and wonder how and why it all happened the way it unfolded but you'll willingly accept the outcome, knowing you made a positive impression. With clarity, you will see what good is done by telling the truth, coming to the conclusion that it was your destination and your destiny.

Preconceived notions will be fractured as you begin to view your old reality with new eyes, and you will question your own perception of free will. Relax. Enjoy the ride. Set your intentions early in life and they will guide the way. Stay motivated. Be resilient. Speak your truth. Rely on instinct. Soul School is a place where the test always precedes the lesson. When you recognize this place as such, once you acknowledge that you have no control, surrender to it. Strive for excellence but forgive yourself the inevitable mistakes.

In spite of the shattered illusions and the disillusionment you will endure, it will all be worth it in the end. Remember, no one is getting out of this classroom alive. Drink the nectar, soak in every moment.

Andrea Perron, author
House of Darkness House of Light

# ISOLATION, EMBARRASSMENT, AND LESS THAN

This week, in 2023, someone asked me to write a letter to my younger self, which seemed like an easy task at face value. After several days of thinking about how I would write this letter to myself and what I would say, I realized that the task was much more challenging than I had imagined. Where would I start?

I decided to write a letter to my twenty-year-old self. The twenty-year-old version of me truly needed a good strong kick in the pants! Yes, a letter to my sixteen-year-old self would probably be more fun, but if I'm completely honest, my sixteen-year-old self wouldn't know what to do with this information. I was too immature and way too confused about—everything. That's why I thought my twenty-year-old self would be a better candidate to make good use of the future knowledge I am about to share. So, let's begin.

Dear Dak,

Yes, it's me... Or rather, you in the future. I've been given this opportunity to write you this letter, so listen up! What I'm about to tell you is important.

First and foremost, we know that there are foundational personality traits that have affected and influenced many of our past and present decisions. Even at 20, you already know you have issues at some level. My first bit of advice is to stop lying about those issues and instead take a hard look at yourself and see what is real. Then address that reality. What? You don't know what I'm talking about? Rubbish! But I'll play along! Let's look at a few of the most life-changing examples.

We left Massachusetts to attend school in Southern California—a smart decision. Good for you! Though we loved being in and from New England, there was too much baggage accumulated at home for us to unpack. Leaving Massachusetts was the only way to move forward and slowly address the bits and pieces. It made sense at the time, and it still makes sense today. Even though leaving everything you knew and starting over all by yourself was hard, you did it. Kudo to you for that decision and for having the perseverance to make a life for yourself in the Golden State.

But dude, I gotta tell you... When we also ran off to the Virgin Islands—not one of our best decisions. This was a knee-jerk reaction to hide from what you thought were failures. You weren't failing; you were unpacking emotional crap and needed time. You had a lot to reconcile, and you put so much pressure on yourself.

I want to take this opportunity to explore why we were so quick to run away because if I'm being honest. Running is still your solution to many problems, and it shouldn't be. Let me begin by telling you that at twenty, you thought you knew more than you did. Like most twenty-year-olds, you were always searching for something! But at fifty-something, and after writing this letter, I realized what we were running from—our shadows. This deep Psychology stuff will make a lot more sense when you get older!

Okay, let's agree that you and I have always spent hundreds of hours in retrospection and introspection. Hate to tell you bud, but that hasn't changed. You'll understand in roughly ten years that we have issues with control. We never understood what aspects of control have affected us the most. But after several days of thinking about this letter, I believe our control issues stem from our first Asthma attack. I don't remember what day it was, how old we were, or even the circumstances that led up to the attack. What I do remember is that we were a slave to our health condition. Remember how we said to our elementary school friends that we must "pay rent for our life?" We had to purchase and take medications every day to stay alive, and no one else we knew had the same experience. We hated being different.

We were lucky because we lived in a community with many other kids our age. Sometimes we played outdoors for hours, but that didn't always go well with our condition. Remember when Peter stopped being our friend because we had an asthma attack while playing baseball? You hit what should have been a home run, but by the time you got to third base, you were in a full-blown asthma attack and had to be taken to the hospital. Or how about that Spring Day when it was windy? A bunch of the neighborhood kids were outside flying kites, but you had to watch from your bedroom window. Spring and Fall were always a nightmare for seasonal allergies, and that year's pollen count was really high.

But it was much more than just playing outside. Remember when the other kids had sleepovers, birthday parties, or played team sports in someone's backyard? You loved to play ice hockey. We couldn't do many of these things because of *asthma*. Stupid Asthma! Stole so much of what you enjoyed and affected how you related to others and how others related to you.

Cats, dust, pollen, you name it, triggered an asthma attack. Every decision we made, every action we took, was always shrouded by the question of whether we'd incur an asthma attack. You hated that, and you hated being known as the sick kid.

Interestingly, someone reading this today would never know that back in the seventies, there weren't the medications available today. Remember that fateful day in the car's back seat when our parents drove from Massachusetts to Northern Maine to see our mom's parents? We must have been in fourth grade. I know you remember this day because it's seared into my memory, which means it was also burned into yours. That was the day our Alupant inhaler stopped working because we had become immune to the drug. We fell to the floor in the back of the car, trying desperately to breathe. We continued inhaling diminishing puffs of that Alupant until we drained the container entirely of its contents. We knelt on the car's floor to lean against the back seat as if we were praying. It was a horrible experience and forged many of the seeds of fear that affect us to this day.

I remember that on that day in the car, we had wished we were never born, and truthfully, we had hoped we would die. We were tired of being different. We were tired of gasping for air. We were tired of not being free to do the things we enjoyed. Most people don't understand how the effects of a chronic illness wear away at your strength and perseverance.

That night, after more than twelve hours of labored breathing, our mother took us to the closest hospital, which was in New Brunswick, Canada. After giving us shots of adrenalin, the attack subsided. The Canadian doctors convinced our mother to put us on high doses of Theophylline and gave us Beclovent and Ventolin inhalers. These medications, which were not yet legal in the United States, probably saved our life. If you recall, another young girl who lived close by experienced asthma as severe as ours. She ultimately died at age twelve. This is likely why we hold Canada and its medical system in such high regard.

Later, when our parents took us back to our pediatrician in Massachusetts, we explained to the doctor that our asthma controls most of our life. We also told the doctor that we should have been allowed to die as an infant. These strong feelings, which you argued were based on nature's law of survival of the fittest, were coupled with our decision never to have biological children of our own. We always said that knowing the illnesses in our family; it would be selfish to spread that gene pool. I never wanted another person ever to feel what I felt—Isolation, embarrassment, and less then.

That day we told the doctor that we had wished for death. So, they put us on a suicide watch. Do you remember hearing the doctor tell our mother? Of course, you do. Because I do; on that day, we decided never to share the truth about our feelings with another person because we feared the words would be used against us. You probably didn't use those terms, but we did keep the important and most sensitive things to ourselves, and we only gave enough information for people to think we were open and honest. We became skilled at sizing up nurses, teachers, and even counselors, mainly to tell them what we were supposed to say and never what was real. It's funny how a well-meaning, single event led to a lifetime of distrust.

We know that the threat of an asthma attack has controlled much of our life. This is probably why we have reacted strongly to other adults who tried to control us. Some well-meaning adults even forced us into positions that led to an asthma attack—like the day we had to go to the nurse's office because the teacher forced us to play dodgeball. Even though we wanted to play, we knew we would end up embarrassed because we would have an asthma attack, which is precisely what happened. Again, we were lucky because our mother was pretty smart. She quickly realized we felt powerless. At another doctor's appointment, our doctor asked Mom questions about us, and she responded by saying, *I don't know, why don't you ask him?* While we didn't realize control over our destiny had become an issue, our mother did. Kudos to Mom for recognizing this!

Unfortunately, others in positions of power—teachers, principals, and other civic officials—did not share our mother's ability to think beyond simplicity. You saw this when one teacher made you stay inside during recess and trapped you between a wall, a bulletin board, and two student desks. She sat in front of you, blocking your escape. You felt the fight-flight response come over you. You picked up one of the desks and threw it at the teacher. Then, you ran out of the school. How about the time you had to go to the principal's office? He lifted you to sit on his desk, leaned over you, placed his hands on your shoulders, and put his face close to yours. Okay, you can stop laughing because you remember kicking him as hard as possible in the privates. As he slumped over in pain, you jumped from the desk and ran out of the school.

It wasn't just officials who made you feel trapped. You also punched your aunt in the breast as hard as possible because she was trying to hold you down. But it wasn't until you jumped out of the third-floor window because your father blocked the doorway that everyone realized your need to escape from feeling trapped was so profound that you could inadvertently kill yourself or seriously hurt someone else. That's when your parents told everyone never to restrain you because of your intense feelings of being trapped. The change in how people treated you ultimately changed your behavioral responses to them, and you became less volatile and more amenable.

I've told you that you were lucky twice. I'm going to reiterate how lucky you are. When you are in your thirties, you will work on the design of a school for children with emotional issues. When you get there and see the kids and hear the teachers and counselors tell you why they were at that school, you'll realize that you were one of these kids. You were lucky that your parents refused to have you labeled. Instead, they found an alternative school based on active learning. They knew you would thrive in an exploratory environment. But more importantly, they knew you needed a school that would allow you to do things differently. I firmly believe that if you had been put in a different school, you would have ended up in prison. Or, perhaps, even dead.

I am confident that our asthma caused us to demand some level of control over our life. When others tried to control us, we reacted the only way we knew how. Unfortunately, even at fifty-something, we tend to be a lone-wolf. You can admit it. We do not let people get too close to us, we are notorious for ghosting others, and we don't often share important things in our lives. Perhaps we can blame our aloofness on Asthma as well.

Aside from not being able to participate fully with our childhood friends, many nights in our early years were spent kneeling on the kitchen chair and leaning over the table, laboring to breathe. Yes, we know this was a regular occurrence. Almost four times a month, we would stay awake all night, unable to breathe. I don't even think Mom and Dad knew just how often this occurred.

While these nights were torturous, what was worse was the attempts by other people to help when we were in a full-blown attack. Do you remember how angry we got when people tried to assist us? As IF they knew what to do? We knew they couldn't do anything. We just had to wait for the attack to pass, which sometimes would take several hours. During this time, all we wanted was to be left alone. This is probably where we learned to retreat and push people away. Yup, I know you push people away in your twenties, and to some degree, you will continue to do so throughout your life. You think you have to deal with everything on your own.

So, there you have it, younger self. These are some of the demons you have carried with you from your youth. What I would like you to do from this day forward is to remember two important events. This first was when you did your first backflip and looked at the ground in mid-air. For that moment in time, you felt freedom. You were not trapped, and you could fly. So, stop running, do a back flip— fly, and know you have more freedom than most. Second, remember what it felt like when we rode a wave for the first time? We synced with the ocean's force and felt part of something bigger than ourselves. Stop trying to do everything on your own if you can work with the amazing power of Mother Nature; you can most certainly work with other people.

Lastly, I want you to seriously consider slowing down, being more honest with yourself, and working with the universe—stop fighting yourself and trust in your abilities. You are lucky because others want to be around you, and many want to help you reach your dreams. Please pay attention to those people, and don't take them for granted. You have all the ingredients to be amazing. You only need to trust and believe. Oh yeah... and wear sunscreen! These damn wrinkles and sunspots really piss me off!

Love,
You, Your Older Self

Dak Kopec
Author of Broken Boys Beyond Friendships

# DEAR ME,

Y<sub></sub>ou're fifteen and you can't control anything going on around you except a few small things in your world. Your days are repetitive. Eat. School. Band. Homework. Home.

Hoping when you come home the house will be quiet. Even when it's vacant, and you're the only soul there, the tension of the adults lingers like the little ghost girl who haunts the halls. You close yourself in your room to ward off the dread, focusing on the minute things you do have power over. But even your room isn't safe.

It's always cold.

The cold lingers when you're under the stacks of blankets or when the sun is baking the house in the summer. Bees buzz in between the window screen and the glass slowly building their hive. You hope the towels you have shoved in the cracks in the frame will keep them from getting into your room. At night you desperately desire to escape the yelling and the noise outside your door from your mother arguing with her latest boyfriend about his kids living with you. They sleep in the living room. Even when all goes quiet you still can't drift off to sleep. Whatever lives in your closet flows out and stands at the end of your bed glaring at you.

He sees you even through the covers.

Even the little ghost girl is terrified of him. It doesn't help the closet door never fully shuts. You can try, but it pops back open. Every fiber of your being hopes you can make it to the weekend until you can escape and go with your grandparents. Until then, you desperately grasp onto your sanity. You pour your time into books, pick up a needle and thread, and start sewing. The steady movement of the needle in and out of the cloth keeps you focused. It's easier to concentrate on the needle instead of the thin blade you keep hidden in your desk drawer.

The sharp edge pressed against flesh. The thin red line, so much like the thread you use, against pale flesh. Sharp pain as it slices along a vein.

Something stops you, and you turn back to the needle slipping in and out of black cloth. The thread is your lifeline from sinking into the darkness and the looming depression hanging over you. It would be so easy to slip deeper into the abyss that awaits and use the razor, but you don't.

You hang on.

\*\*\*

Hang on.

It's the one thing I could go back and tell my fifteen-year-old self. The darkness isn't encompassing. You do break away from the shadows hovering over your life. You leave the house behind with all its problems. You find yourself. It can be tough, and you might want to give in but don't. There is a light no matter if you can't see it.

Keep on sewing. Keep on sinking into your imagination and grasp onto the things you love to get you through. Embrace the gifts the gods have given you and face the fear. Know that people love and care for you. No matter how hard it gets.

Hang on.

Love me.
Crymsyn Hart.
Author

# HEY WADE,

I'm addressing this letter to eleven-year-old you. I know things aren't too good for you there in 1983 except on the weekends, so hopefully this will help you get through the next few years until you get your driver's license.

I'm writing from the year 2023. Yes, really. And I've got good news and bad news. The good news, George Lucas makes more *Star Wars* movies. The bad news is, George Lucas makes more *Star Wars* movies.

I won't spoil anything else for you. But the fact that I got here from where you're at should tell you that things go really well for the most part.

I know you're not much of a reader at this point in your life, so instead of giving you an essay that you'll toss in favor of the latest issue of *Heavy Metal*, I would like to offer you forty pieces of wisdom, one for each of the years in between my now and yours:

      1. If you want something, just ask. All they can do is say no.

2. Speaking of, it's okay for you to say no. Seriously.

3. Your parents really do want the best for you. But sometimes you know better than they do what that is.

4. People are going to die. Don't take your time with them for granted.

5. Don't postpone joy.

6. Be vigilant against emotional vampires.

7. You're not as smart as you think you are. But you're smarter than *they* think you are.

8. We suffer more in imagination than we do in reality.

9. Don't forget Momma's birthday. It's July 5. Every year.

10. The main villain? She hates herself way more than she hates you.

11. Yes, school sucks, but you need to try a little harder.

12. All the nerdy shit you like becomes cool shit. Just give it about three decades.

13. I know you switch from Art to Drafting in a couple of years. I don't want to talk you out of that because it works out. But maybe take Drafting in addition to Art.

14. That creative writing assignment Mrs. Clifford gives you in eighth grade, you'll love it. Dive in.

15. Style is the stuff you get wrong (re: #14).

16. See if you can remember if you really saw that UFO. Your memory of it is a whole lot fresher than mine.

17. Don't go into debt any more than absolutely necessary.

18. Don't let the bastards wear you down.

19. Don't take it so personally.

20. Don't limit yourself.

21. Read Teddy Roosevelt's *The Man in the Arena*.

22. They're just jealous. For real.

23. It's okay to be scared. Do it anyhow.

24. Yes, you can be a weirdo sometimes. Own it.

25. Reading is fun, it's just that the stuff they make you read in school is not.

26. You're going to feel like a choirboy for abstaining from drugs and alcohol when all your friends aren't. Know that it was always the right decision.

27. The obstacle is the way.

28. It doesn't matter what anyone else thinks. (You're still struggling with this one.)

29. Maybe soft-pedal that rebel flag redneck shit.

30. It's okay to listen to bands that don't have big hair and wear spandex.

31. The best answer to anger is silence.

32. The greatest remedy for anger is delay.

33. You have power over your mind, not outside events.

34. When you're scared to tackle something new, think of it this way: there is somebody out there who has done this with half your intelligence and skill because they wanted it more than you.

35. If you want to improve, be content to be thought foolish.

36. Go to that Rush concert you get invited to. It will be your last chance until 2007.

37. Don't wait until you're in your twenties to get back into comic books. And make sure you're reading DC stuff no later than 1986.

38. Get tested for Factor V Leiden at some point before 2020.

39. Make good art.

40. Memento mori, man. Memento mori.


Wade Beauchamp
(Author)

# FROM 89-YEAR-OLD DWIGHT TO 19-YEAR-OLD DWIGHT

Dwight, you are a smart, nice-looking kid whom many people like. But you have this inner fear and loathing of yourself for what you believe to be unnatural and sinful inclinations. All through high school, you wondered why you found pictures of naked men more exciting than pictures of naked women; why you were more aroused by boys in low-riding Levis than by girls in tight sweaters; why your movie star fantasies involved Robert Mitchum, Burt Lancaster, and Kirk Douglas rather than Jane Russell, Hedy Lamarr, and Marilyn Monroe; why you had that crush on the high school football coach. You've been taught by your religion that homosexuality and masturbation are mortal sins punishable by eternal torment. You've been told by the civil authorities that homosexual acts are criminal offenses punishable by imprisonment. You have repressed this integral part of yourself, fearing social ostracism and legal punishment if you admitted to being what you are.

Well, Dwight, these feelings are not unnatural, sinful, or disgusting. You are part of a small but significant minority of people who, through genetic and hormonal processes not of their choosing, happen to be sexually attracted to persons of their own sex. You are not diseased or wicked.

During the immediate coming years, you will find yourself under intense pressure from family and peers to marry and have children. You need to resist these pressures, as marriages between gay and straight people tend to fail. Gayness can be repressed, but it can never be eliminated; it will always be lurking in the background. Marriage to a straight person will not "cure" homosexuality, because homosexuality is not a disease. Probably the main objection to homosexuals is that they do not produce children like "normal" people; in today's overcrowded world, that objection is senseless.

As time goes on, you will become increasingly skeptical about religion, and eventually, you will abandon it. You will come to appreciate evolution and the laws of nature as adequate explanations for the wonders of the universe.

In days to come, people like you will become organized and demand their civil rights. You will no longer be classed as a criminal and will enjoy equal legal privileges with straight people. You will learn to accept yourself for what you are and to enjoy your sexual leanings. You will meet many people who feel just as you do, and you will find joy in several intimate and long-term same-sex relationships. You will end up living in a community where people accept you for what you are, and you will come to regard yourself as gifted, rather than cursed. You have a long life ahead of you, Dwight, so be yourself and make the most of it.

Dwight Fine

# DEAR CHRIS,

This letter contains the five most important pieces of advice you'll never read.

You can't read it. You don't exist anymore.

If I could somehow reach you where you are now and hand you this letter, would that be the best thing for you? Would it help you for the better?

I honestly don't know. As much as I want to change what's going to happen to you, change the decisions people will make that will irreversibly harm you, and stop you from making decisions that will harm yourself... who knows what would happen if you didn't suffer those consequences?

Would you be better off facing the world without those experiences, or are you better prepared for the world because of them? Would you be the person you are now, or would you be someone with less to heal? Or would you need more healing in other ways?

I want to protect you. You deserve to be protected from the harmful realities of the world. But I don't know if that's most helpful to you. Honestly, exposing you to the harshness of the world may help you gain critical coping skills to deal with what's coming your way.

Who's to say what the best course forward would be?

Luckily, I don't have to worry about it. While I'm writing this to a twelve-year-old me, that poor kid will never read it. I will, however. And I will continue to read this for years to come.

At this point in my life, I have some things to say that I wish my preteen self could have heard and damn the consequences.

I want to address something you have been denying about yourself. I think directness is something you appreciate, but it will also be difficult for you to hear.

You are gay. Homosexual. Queer, as you will later prefer being called, because it's more inclusive of the identities you will find describe you.

You are a person who will grow up and be attracted to men. You're attracted to them right now. We both know it. And I get it. It's scary. So terrifying, especially given the world you live in.

You will be okay. *Know* that you will be okay. Don't just believe it. *Know* it.

You see, you just need some support and love. To that end, I hope you'll forgive me for discussing some painful things about your life while you're in this spot. But I want to make sure you know that I understand where you are, so you'll believe me when I say you're going to be okay.

**First**, please don't stay stuck in the fear of what's already changed.

Which is you. *You've* changed. But you're afraid no one will love you for this change. Understandable. It will take some time for you to understand the nuances of the love your parents have for you, but you will have it. Always.

In the same way you know you're gay, you know something's wrong in the home you're growing up in. You can't place your finger on it, but that's because it's beyond your understanding of the complexities of human nature. You're twelve, after all. You don't even know how to drive yet, so how can you possibly understand the way adults process the emotions from their childhood trauma?

Your parents love you. Not in the ways you want them to. They don't always express it in the best ways, but they've got your back when it comes down to it. You will need to learn self-love, while still recognizing you are worthy of love from others. You don't deserve to have your parent's lack of coping skills translate into your abuse, and it's also true that people can be forgiven when they learn what they didn't know before.

**Second**, blood may be thicker than water, but all that means is that it's harder to wash it out of the fabric of your life.

Your brother's abuse is unacceptable, and you don't deserve it. Your parents don't know how bad it is. And I understand it's confusing because you keep telling them you're in pain, and they keep dismissing it as normal.

It's not normal. It's manipulation to the utmost degree, and you'll need some time to unravel from the lies he's sold you. And, as soon as you can, cut him out of your life. He only causes you confusion and pain with his gaslighting and harmful decisions.

**Third**, do what you want to do.

Seriously. You love telling stories, so be an actor. Be a novelist, a playwright, a poet, and a screenwriter. Be all the things you want to be but never thought you could be!

That also means moving. You want to move, so do it! The hell with student loan costs, your fears and doubts. Apply for those schools. Try the University of Utah or Boise State! Go big!

But that means buckling down in school. Don't worry about being popular. What good will that do in the long run? People your age won't remember you for being popular. They'll remember you if you were kind, helpful, and made them laugh.

**Fourth**, with all that being said, draw some boundaries through learning self-advocacy.

You're not a doormat. You're not the type of person a guy would just settle for, who would only deign to be with you. You are desirable, and you need to believe it. This means you'll want to take care of yourself, show yourself the love you know you're worthy of receiving, because you give it so fiercely.

You could spend your whole life trying to be the person you think everyone wants you to be, or the person you think you *should* be. But who sets those standards? A society ruled by white men who, time after time, demonstrate their unwillingness to change what doesn't work for minorities because it works so well for them?

Stand up and stand proud against them. You are a passionate, loving, driven queer person, and you are absolutely irreplaceable in all the ways that matter. The fire inside you can serve as a beacon of hope or can burn the world to ashes. Choose good, even if it is a little chaotic now and then.

**Fifth**, but not because it's least important: slow down and relax.

You're one tense kid. You don't know it now, but you tell a lot of jokes to make people laugh because you're trying to cover up your fears of inadequacy. It's valid, and it's relatable. But it's ultimately unnecessary.

See, some people won't like you. Some people will hate you. And there is *absolutely nothing* you can do about it. It's nothing you've done wrong. It's your existence. And, honestly, why would you *ever* apologize to someone for existing? Don't. Don't ever do it. Stand proud and firm in the knowledge of your worth as a human.

After all is said and done, just remember to find your joy. And, most importantly, I hope you remember it's been in you all along.

With all the love I carry,

Chris Cole
(Author)

# DEAR PAST PATRICK,

Today was the day your dream almost died. Talking with your creative writing teacher and him telling you that you've got no talent and should give up writing stops you in your tracks. I know how much you respect his opinion, and he has a long list of publications. I know how much this hurt and understand why you walked away from writing.

Did you notice the almost in the first sentence?

Would you believe you've written and published twelve books?

It's true.

Where you are now, you are dealing with a lot of bad stuff. You value others' opinions of you far more than you value yourself. Years of trauma and abuse have pushed you to a place where you don't trust yourself. Your "friends" use you, then drop you when it isn't convenient. Your family criticizes everything you do. It's only natural that you've gotten here. It is okay to feel down and despondent, for a bit.

There is one exception to this. Dad has always been your light in the dark. Listen to him more. He's the one person who's never let you down, never made you feel less than good enough, or stupid for trying new things. He's not just being "nice". He loves you and goes out of his way to make things better. All these years later, he's still an inspiration and role model for us.

What I've learned since the day you gave up on being an author is that people, intentionally or not, criticize others to make themselves feel better. Taking risks that they fear to take gets a warning. Success, where they have failed, brings ridicule or criticism. Some people are just damaged and can't be happy for others no matter the accomplishment. They are also the first ones to brag about your accomplishments to others to make themselves seem important.

What should you do?

Follow your dreams, and better yet, chase down the things that scare the fuck out of you. Rejection won't kill you, I promise. The things we most want are the things you are afraid that you will fail at. And guess what?

YOU WILL FAIL.

You will fail many times, sometimes in a spectacular way. Does it hurt, hell yes. Is it worth it, hell yes. Every failure is a teaching experience. You will learn far more from your failures than from your successes. When you finally achieve your goals, you will look back, as I am doing now, and rejoice that we took the chance, laid it all on the table, and took our shot. Our best moments in life come from these failed experiments. We do this every day in the lab. When your classmate mixed the wrong reagents and almost poisoned everyone in the room, you jumped in and got it into the hood where it was contained. The twenty other things that blew up and went wrong prepared you for that event. It is the same in life.

At the end of the day, I am really proud of you. We have survived many situations that could have ended badly. We have fought through terrible times to make it to a life that is far happier than I ever expected. It took strength, courage, and help from some amazing people to achieve the dreams that we've had since we were little, but achieve them we did, and every day, we achieve new things that we never thought possible.

My final thought is believe in yourself because few others do. Fight for causes that are important to you. Oh, and invest all your money in Microsoft stock. I'd really appreciate it.

Future Patrick
2023
Patrick Dugan
Author

# THE NIGHT WE WENT TO HELL (AND DIDN'T CARE)

To understand my letter to my past, you need some background. Quite a bit of it, really, considering how different my world was to yours....

It was a shabby and narrowly-focused time in a shabby and narrow place: 1963, in the ancient city of York, in the poverty-stricken northern English county of Yorkshire.

Too long ago and far away, you might be thinking. So foreign and distant in every sense that it could never reach out to you and take you back there. But I'm here to show that it can. And it will.

Come with me into that shabby, down-at-heel world. Not even twenty years after World War Two, Old York's soot-caked streets still had yawning, darkened gaps where Nazi bombs had destroyed homes and lives.

There had never been much money on my side of the tracks, between the smelly chocolate factory and the glorious medieval cathedral, known as York Minster. Where I lived, we were close to the slums proper, and lived in constant fear of tipping over the edge to join them.

It was a world that is almost indescribable even to young Brits today, to whom my home city is now a sort of Roman/Viking/medieval theme park thrumming with tourists who gawp at ancient houses and alleys that could have come straight out of Harry Potter. In my day the glitz and gloss had yet to come; the history that surrounded me was heavy, sour, and sullen, not shiny and welcoming.

My world was narrow. But I wasn't. I was a big, big girl, hideously aware of being fat and ugly – as I saw myself – a view that was mercilessly reinforced by many people who saw my self-disgust as an invitation to abuse me. When you're down, there's nothing some people like more than giving you a good kicking.

But into my shabby, black-and-white world had come some glamour and excitement. I'd become a Mormon convert and gloried in the feeling of being one of God's chosen, one of the few who knew the truth and belonged to the only true Christian church on Earth. And part of my new life involved spending most of my spare time at the shiny new, American-style church-house on the other side of town, which even boasted the sort of shiny new kitchen – the local women said in hushed tones, "It's *all-electric!*," unlike their own dank and dismal sculleries with pre-war gas ovens and dim lighting. The American kitchen even boasted a tall, glossy fridge, just like the ones in Hollywood movies. It was all so glamorous, and even I was part of it.

Also, against all the odds, I had a boyfriend. Jeff, slightly older and already working – I was still at high school - but like me, a local Mormon convert. Unlike me, though, he was tall and thin, with a riot of red hair and that odd ability to be so funny as to render others helpless with hysteria. Of course, I loved him. We got on brilliantly, reveling in the slight naughtiness of being told off by outraged Mormon elders at the Saturday night dances for our wild and sexy moves.

Wild and sexy though our dance moves might have been, in reality, we just held hands and went about companionably together, nothing more. We loved visiting the local Theatre Royal, where the professional repertory company put on a different play every week – though quite how the actors managed this phenomenal feat of memory still boggles the mind.

And Jeff and I talked. And talked. And talked. Inevitably we found ourselves in the dangerous territory of increasingly questioning the weird and demanding religion we'd volunteered for. Even though the 1960s' British society in general was sexist anyway, I rebelled against the Mormon expectation that I'd marry and bring up vast numbers of kids. Even at my most fanatical, I told the other women – the 'sisters' – that no, I wanted no part of that. I was heading for university. They were outraged, and called me "unnatural."

But Jeff and I had problems with the weird and exclusive theology, too. The seeds were already sown for some kind of ultimate showdown. Little did we realize it would take quite such a dramatic turn.

One day Jeff blurted out to me that he thought – or rather, feared - he was gay. In those days it really wasn't something that involved pride. It took a lot of courage even to tell me about it, his great mate and confidante. But then he decided that, like good Mormon youth are supposed to, to take his "problem" to the elders – specifically the local Bishop. So Jeff made an appointment for one late winter's afternoon to see the Bishop and promised to come over to my place immediately afterwards to tell me all about it.

So there I was, agog and waiting for him that night. But time passed... Jeff should have been over by then, but no... more time passed... the buses might be running late because of the weather.... It was snowing hard...

Eventually, I opened the door to a sodden, sobbing wreck. Jeff had walked all the way across York in the driving snow, crying his heart out. Why?

Oh, God, why do you think...

He'd hesitatingly explained his strong feelings of attraction to men to the Bishop – but had been cut off abruptly. Face red with fury and contorted with disgust, this much-admired pillar of the community yelled: "You are so evil God will never forgive you! No amount of prayer or repentance will help you! You are polluting my office! Get out and go to Hell where you belong, you unnatural spawn of Satan!"

*Unnatural* – just as the Mormon women had described *me*.

My beloved friend Jeff, who had in all humility put himself in that situation, not surprisingly crumbled under this vile and vehement attack by the much older authority figure. At the very least, Jeff had expected to be heard out, perhaps even partly supported by some sort of father figure, but instead, he'd had the door slammed on him both literally and figuratively.

That night, Jeff hadn't even thought of getting a bus but had slogged on by foot through the snow and wind all the way over to see me, an utter emotional wreck.

I sat him in front of the hot coal fire, rubbed his soaking red hair with a towel, and comforted him. But all the while something was bubbling up in me – a mixture of outrage and fury, yes, but surely something else, too.

The something else, I now realize, was *power*. Gone was the miserable, self-hating girl, and in her place suddenly was a decisive powerhouse.

"Come on, Jeff!" I found myself saying briskly. "We've had our doubts about that weird religion for ages now. Look, this is IT. This is where we break away. Let's just leave the awful Mormon Church and never, ever go back."

He looked up, red-rimmed eyes suddenly bright and even a bit mischievous. The old Jeff was back.

"What shall we do?" he asked.

Whatever we did next had to be utterly non-Mormon, a symbolic quitting: THE END. We had quite a choice as they're against a lot, including coffee and tea, sex outside marriage, and smoking and drinking. Seeing as falling into bed with each other wasn't on the cards and celebrating our freedom with a pot of coffee never occurred to us anyway, to me there was only one answer.

"Let's go to a pub – *and have a drink*," I suggested, knowing as I said it that the deal was already done. I was fully aware that to Mormons we were going to Hell, but I didn't care then - and I've never cared since. To me, the real sinners are those who cause others pain and humiliation for simply being who they are. I was willing to take my chance on Hell, kid though I was.

As it was still only early evening, there was plenty of time to strike out in our new rebellion against that most Puritan of religions.

We wandered towards the center of town through the lessening snow past a couple of pubs but didn't really like the look of them.

"I know," said the newly irrepressible Lynn, "Let's go to the Theatrical Pub."

This was a place near the Minster called York Arms and yes, it was indeed where the actors from the Theatre Royal would congregate after (and sometimes before) their performances around the corner. But – and you might have been ahead of me here – it was also the gay pub. Neither Jeff nor I was aware of this, though we soon would be.

It goes without saying that Jeff's new life took off that night.

It was to end a few years ago, when he died in his husband's arms at their home in Sweden, after a long and happy life together.

And on that momentous night so long ago, I made several lifelong friends, the first steps in becoming the proud gay ally I am so obviously today.

All of which is a very long introduction to my letter back to the Lynn of that night, which surely has to go like this:

"My darling Teenage Me,

You've just done something remarkable, kid. You've broken with a cult that's proved itself to be not only nonsensical but also vile and inhumane. You've defended your best friend and encouraged him to accept himself for what he is. You've been super strong and impressive. And you're just sixteen. (We'll overlook the fact you were an illegally underage drinker!)

If only you could somehow distil that feeling of decisiveness, of power, and keep it in you through all the long years afterwards. If only you could switch the love and understanding you've just shown Jeff to yourself!

And now you are me... If only *I* could have found the strength to support *myself* with such tiger-like passion as I did him that night.

But you, you have it all before you, all those ups and downs... Whatever you do, whatever happens, hang onto that strength and never forget it. See yourself as the hero you are, not as a big, wobbly girl who might as well go around with a sign saying "Kick Me" on your back. Retrieve and reclaim the sheer cocky confidence of that night. Do it. You won't regret it.

You will be strong again. You will be inspired – and inspire many others – and you'll be successful. You will write the truth about religion and reach a global audience. (You will even be thin!)

But it's been tough. It would have been much easier if you'd have remembered and called upon the sheer positive energy you summoned that snowy night in 1963 for Jeff but also now *for yourself, and* do it over and over. Jeff was worthy of love and support, but so were you.

You are a hero and a star. And never, ever, forget it.

With all love and biggest, warmest, and most supportive hugs, from 76-year-old Lynn (who is still working, still fighting against Mormon persecution of gay people – oh still wearing leather trousers and bright red lipstick. And I won't give up.)

By Lynn Picknett

Writer, editor, and co-author of several non-fiction books, including *The Templar Revelation* (1997) with Clive Prince, which inspired *The Da Vinci Code*. They were given cameo roles in the movie. Freelance editor for Gold Dust Publishing, LLC.

# DEAR PAISLEY,

Y ou will struggle growing up feeling awkward, different, and confused by the way you feel. You will have a difficult time with your family understanding and accepting who you are. You will face many challenges; losing basically every family member that you were ever close to. A creative outlet called drag will be in your future. It gives you the freedom to be whoever you want and choose your own gay family.

Paisley, you will make many friends and acquaintances along the way and have a long drag career. However, you will suffer a lot of internal unhappiness. Because you choose to not be the person you were meant to be. You will be afraid of what people think instead of making yourself happy. You will suffer from depression and battle an eating disorder. There will be a time when you are at your breaking point and will finally live for yourself. However, a bright light will be at the end of the tunnel.

You will finally come out as a transgender woman in the second half of your life. You will have a wonderful doctor who will help you with your journey. Your drag family and the community you have been a part of will open their hearts and minds to you and be supportive. That scared little boy who used to pray at night that he would wake up and be the girl she was meant to be, will blossom into a successful adult woman. Your hope and happiness will be restored.

Paisley, your journey won't be easy. But I promise you, you will become who you were meant to be.

With love,
Paisley Taylor
Paisley Parque

# TO THE GIRL HIDING IN THE CORNER,

You're not insane. Those song lyrics running through your head on repeat when the world was crashing and burning, the poetry you washed in the sink with globs of Dawn because you thought it was soiled, the shoes you threw at the creature from your imagination, none of it was trying to hurt you. They were all messages from your brain.

Do you remember how you had to go to the fourth floor of the school library, push a divided desk into the corner, remove all your rings, and stow your belongings in the next cubicle just so you could study? And how you still ended up answering the scrawled messages on the cubicle walls instead of reading your textbooks? How about how you had to rederive all the equations in Physics class rather than memorizing them? Do you remember how you had to turn the things you needed to recall into songs in order for them to stick? Or how about the fact that you just had to stop writing this letter and read everything up to this point aloud to decipher what the hell you were trying to say?

You know how, when you're in a crowded room, you are not only hearing it all as a jumbled ball of sound but also feeling everyone around you as various spikes and troughs of energy to the point of system overload? How you zero in on whatever music is playing - even if you hate it - because it makes everything else shut the fuck up?

You see those scars every day - the ones from when you felt like you had so much inside, you had to let it out. They're not evidence of your damage, they're a reminder of your humanity. It's natural for you to feel a compulsion once you find something that gives you the endorphins that your brain doesn't.

You are not broken.

They call this ADHD, but it's so much more than whatever connotation you have when you hear that acronym. It's not some new, made-up condition, it's not some fad that people use to hide from personal accountability, and it's certainly not an excuse to be lazy. You are far from lazy. If you don't believe your future self, look around at all you've already accomplished.

But you do lose your phone at least three times a day. That disorganized shelf that's been bothering the hell out of you every time you sit on the couch? You forget to ever straighten it. And yes, at forty-one years old, you're still going to be going back to restaurants to retrieve your credit card from the booklet you left it in.

I wish this message could travel through time so you could understand that the pressure building up inside of you begging for release isn't all the feelings, information, and energy you've absorbed, despite how it feels. It's anxiety. You're terrified of missing, forgetting, or misplacing something important. That fear will push you to accomplish much, but there's a cost. The anxiety will begin to become debilitating later in life when you refuse to give in to your unhealthy outlets because you have people who need you to keep it together.

But it's okay!

Because your life is going to be pretty damn awesome.

Your search for healthier outlets will pay off. You're going to create so much—fantasy stories, little forces of nature disguised as children, art that you forget to hang, beautiful gardens that you forget to weed. You are going to impact people around you—hurt some, inspire others, but most importantly, connect. You're going to find a supportive partner who helps to diffuse your inner bomb. Not only are you not broken, but you are far from alone. There are entire communities of people who understand what this feels like.

Be kind to yourself. Stop calling yourself a dingbat, idiot, or worse, especially when you have a daughter who is wired like you are. She is none of those things, and you know in your heart that you aren't either.

So, stay in the corner if you like. Dance to the music that other people can't hear, add to the collection of disfigured paperclips on your desk, bite the hell out of your #2 pencils until they look like beaver chews, and fill your notes with sketches of dragons and pyramids. You might not be like everyone else around you, but that's also why you shine.

Love, Me

P.S. Keep writing. Your path won't follow the map you've got in your head, but you're going to be published multiple times over.

Sarah J. Sover
Author

# TO MY BARELY TWELVE-YEAR-OLD SELF,

The first thing that I need to say is that I wish that I could be there to wrap my arms around you and shield you from all the pain that you're suffering. You deserve protection and love. You did nothing to deserve the years of abuse and neglect that you have gone through and that will sadly continue for more. I know you've had times when you felt that you just couldn't endure anymore. I'm glad that our six-year-old arms were too short to reach that shotgun trigger when you wanted to stop the pain by ending your life. That is a failure that I'm thankful for, as it allowed me to be here today. I know that you won't give up after that and you'll keep silently fighting even if that simply means surviving when you want to die. Please believe me when I say that living will be worth it, because the abuse does eventually end, and your life does get better.

Someday you will understand and believe that you did the right thing by opening up to someone about how they were hurting you at home. I'm sorry to say that it will only temporarily stop the abuse, and unfortunately, it will be worse when it begins again. When your father decides to take his own life, know that it's not because you told someone what they were doing to you, no matter what your mother tells you. You will never fully know why any of them did the things they are doing but you are not responsible for any of their actions. You speaking out about the abuse will be the catalyst for you learning to stand up for yourself.

Over time your self-worth will grow even if you can't comprehend believing it right now. You are more than just something for others to use and abuse with no regard to what you feel or want. Though your physical "virginity" was taken from you, it doesn't mean that you are damaged, unclean, or unworthy, and some people will tell you that. I know that you'll scrub yourself raw with bleach but no matter how hard you try it will never make you feel "clean". YOU'RE NOT DIRTY, THEY ARE!

Even though your "innocence" and the right to choose what is done to your body was taken from you against your will, in time you will learn that you're allowed to say no. You will have boyfriends who will take advantage of your lack of self-worth and inability to set boundaries, and one will add new types of abuse upon you. But there will also be a few that will be kind, they just won't see that you don't understand your right to say no to them. One will finally realize that and tell you something that will shake your very foundation. He will tell you that nothing physical is required to happen until you are ready and want to. He will also be the reason you finally leave your abusive family, not by force or threat, but by refusing to leave you there alone when you tell him to go without you. This is when the abuse finally ends for good. You will still have hard times and bad times, but this is when you start seeing them balance with easy moments and good times.

I am so proud of you, your resilience, your strength, and your ability to still have compassion after all that you have been through. You may feel all alone right now but you do find a "family" that will accept and love you just as you are, not out of pity or in spite of your past. A woman will come into your life who will be the mother to you that you always deserved, and she will stay by your side no matter how complicated the situation becomes. Some relationships will be temporary while others will continue over the decades and each one will hold a place in your heart. This will be your chosen family that teaches you how to trust and love yourself. They will be there for you in your times of need to comfort or help with no strings attached. They will encourage you and be proud of your accomplishments and growth. They will still stand by you when you make mistakes and love you unconditionally. They will appreciate it when you do these things for them as well. This is how you'll learn what "healthy" love and relationships are supposed to be.

We've had a long ride with many ups and downs. You survive through so much and each struggle makes you stronger and wiser over the years. You will never be grateful for what you went through as it did not "make you what you are", you will become what you will be in spite of what you went through. But you will be grateful for how you can use your experiences to help others in the future who are suffering through some of the same things. We are still healing and growing, and I hope that never ends. We are still working on leaving our ashes of the past where they belong, in the past, gone but not forgotten. We are the phoenix burning brightly into whatever the future holds.

I love you little one, I'll be right here waiting for you with open arms.

Sincerely,
Your Future Self.
Mary M.

# DEAR SIX-YEAR-OLD ME,

I see you standing there on that Saturday afternoon in the Piggly Wiggly grocery store where you and your mother queued up in line behind a large white woman and her little boy. He was a little younger than you with freckles and red hair and that beautiful smile that children get when everything in the world is new and wonderful. His name might have been Bobby. He sat atop the grocery basket seat and looked back at you, the way children do when fascinated by another child their age. His mother briefly noticed it while unloading her groceries onto the conveyor belt and frowned disapprovingly. She continued unloading her groceries and Bobby giggled and reached his hand out to you.

"Stop playing with that dirty nee-gra!" his mother scolded him. Your own mother instinctively grabbed your hand and pulled you closer. There is not much more that she could do in Birmingham Alabama in 1961, where history and the strict laws of racial apartheid gave that woman license to openly hate. It will not be the last time that a racial epithet will be cavalierly thrown at you and the racial hatred was something that your mother had known all her life growing up in the segregated Dixie south. But it was this single moment that mixed childlike wonder and adult hatred that will haunt you for a long, long time. Perhaps it was because there was something else you discovered about yourself in the forbidden fruit of Bobby's outreaching hand.

A decade later your family will move to a northern city. After years of non-violent protests to try to change laws that legalized racial discrimination (often met with murderous responses) it was time to find a better place for you to grow into manhood. For the first time, you will go to school with boys who look like Bobby – compete in the same schoolyard games and go to integrated proms and house parties. You will excel in school and begin to be judged by the content of your character, which is so many wonderful things other than the color of your skin. No one will call you a "nee-gra" again, but micro-aggressions and misjudgment of your abilities will still haunt you for many years. But this northern "oasis" will also be a place where Black identity becomes defined as much by poverty, drugs, gangs, and rap music as it does by achievement, progress, and civil rights anthems.

You will travel to many places abroad that will provide you with a respite from the burdens of racial identity. As a teenager, you will travel with an integrated show choir all over Italy, be applauded by Italian audiences, and share gelatos and cannoli with Italian teenagers. You will live in the home of a white French family as an exchange student and just be another one of the kids. After college, you will work in a West African village where effeminate men will have a place of honor as those who are honored as divine healers with feminine and masculine energy. Later in life, you will travel to Vietnam where young people will stare at you, but in a kind of innocent child-like awe, like Bobby did. Perhaps they hark back to a memory of a young Black American soldier or a badass that they saw on MTV. You will encounter other Americans on your travels in Latin America and elsewhere. Those middle-class white Americans treat you with kinship and respect, either out of the perceived commonality of culture or a need to show a better side of the American character as they travel abroad. Each time the US immigration officer says, "Welcome home," your heart will sink as the burden of racial code-switching becomes more obvious and absurd.

One day, when you reach the ripe old age of twenty-nine, you will meet a fair-haired man with sparkling blue eyes and a killer smile. Happenstance will put you together carrying a banner at a gay rights demonstration, which will be followed by many dates, dinners, and kisses. When the time is right, he will invite you to dinner with his widowed mother and sister in an all-white suburban community in a nearby state. Although he prepared them before your arrival, their visual disapproval of his Black boyfriend will not be well-hidden as you entered the house. You will share a polite meal together, punctuated by awkward questions and silences. In future calls, his mother will make it clear that the only thing worse than the shame of having a gay son was the idea of her only son having a Black boyfriend. "How could you do this to me?" she will cry. You were back in that Piggly Wiggly line again. But fortunately, this Bobby has a voice and will make some choices. He will insist on his right to choose whom he will love, even at the risk of alienating his dear mother. Over the next few years, there will be many battles between him and his family, and he will try to shield you from some of it. Even as sickness takes over his body, he will insist on honoring your choices and your relationship. You will love him deeply through sickness and beyond – holding vigil until he breathes his last breath. His mother will ask to accompany you to scatter his ashes over a waterfall in Hawaii and the two of you will have your own intimate ceremony to share different memories of how you loved him. Your relationship with her will continue until she passes away.

You will have other loves in your life. Men with different skin tones, ages, sizes, emotional baggage, and personalities. You will meet men who grew up in the toxic culture of systemic racism. Some will deny their privilege, and some will be conscious of it. You will look deep into the eyes of Black men who share your heritage, pain, and joy without needing words of explanation. You will be embraced by White arms who casually slip in a vile racial suggestion in the throes of passion to arouse their own sexual fantasies. You will nibble on the ears of bi-racial men hungering for a sense of identity and belonging through the exchange of a passionate kiss. Don't worry, over time you will develop the tools to discern which men's affections come from hearts that can unite with your soul and you will learn to hold onto them.

So, young boy, as you watch Bobby with freckles and red hair being pushed away in the grocery cart seat, check to see if he is still looking back, still hoping to make a connection with you. And just maybe, years from now Bobby will turn out to be one of those men who can love another man just for the beautiful human on the inside.

Lorenz Qatava
Palm Springs, CA

# HELLO LINDSEY,

You and I are not acquainted with one another; however, I am your older self. I am going to watch you go through a great many events in your life. Some will be good, and some will not. You are just a young kid right now trying to find your way in this world. You know you are different, but right now you do not fully comprehend how. You feel like you are an outsider in your life. As if you do not quite belong anywhere. Once you start school you will realize just how different you are. You'll be awkward, you'll have a hard time making new friends, and worst of all you'll come to the realization that you are effeminate. Oh, that's not the word that will be used though. You'll be called a sissy, some people will call you Sue, and some will just turn away from you and ignore you. It is not going to be easy for you. You'll find your retreat from this world in old movies. That fascination will shape your whole being to the point that you model your life after those old movies and movie stars. It will become a double-edged sword in part. You will have an escape from the horrific bullying that you receive, but you will start building a fantasy world around yourself as a fortress. It will not take you long to realize that old sepia-toned movies with soundtracks flowing like golden honey are not a true reflection of reality, though you will carry that escapism with you for the rest of your days on this earth.

High School will be the place where you receive the starkest and most horrific of bullying. You will allow yourself to feel less than others because you now know why you are different and those days are not like today as there are support groups, openly gay role models, and it is talked more openly about that during this time for you. It is in this environment that you will learn to fight, not physically, but for your sanity. There will not be a day that goes by that you are not taunted, and you will always remember the name, face, and look of the first person who walked up to you and spoke the F word, "Hey, faggot face." Almost forty years after you graduate you will see him for the first time, and he will recognize you and try to get your attention as if he wants to speak to you. You will feel the rage of a thousand hells rise in your throat as you just walk past him, out of the door of the store, get into your car, turn up the volume of the radio, and fly as fast as you can down highway fourteen, with Cher blaring out of the speakers back to your home in Greensboro. This is the place that at one time seemed so far away from your beginnings in Rockingham County. It would eventually be your escape from what you perceived as a small-town mentality and a bed rife with hurt.

However, let's go back a decade or two. You are out of school, but you still carry the pain of your experiences. You carry it with you as if it is an old worn piece of luggage, weighing you down and constantly there on your journey in this life. You are going to fall into a great many experiences, some will be good, and some will just be the opposite, but you will try your best to make your way. One event in your life that will be the lowest point you ever will have. You will be feeling unloved, unwanted in society, and so emotionally immature that you fall prey to someone who promises to always take care of you, always be there for you, someone who promises you the world, and in the same turn targets your nonexistent self-esteem. He'll convince you that the way to get your power back is to sell your own body. This is in no way a condemnation of someone who freely enters that walk of life. You will give him the power and allow him to control your mind and your body. He will see that hurt little boy you still carry and pounce on the chance to control you. So yes, you will start working for him as a prostitute. Good to his word though, he is always there sitting outside the cheap hotel rooms waiting for you to emerge, money in hand, and just a bit more of your soul, to hand over to him. One night it will all go awry, and you find yourself in a situation - behind that door. You will do just as you have been told to do to signal for help. You will pick up the nearest thing to you and throw it through the window of that cheap room. As it is happening you will not realize it, but that chair will be the weapon that breaks through to a new future. You escape and your pimp meets you as you are running across the parking lot to his "safety". With his utterance of, "What the fuck happened?" You will say nothing, but look dead at him and begin to walk, and then run away from him and that life. The bastion that you will so carefully build around yourself will fall away at that very minute in shards just like the cascade of broken glass from that window. Somehow in the melee of that happening a small bit of that glass ends up in the upturned cuff of your jeans. You'll put that little remembrance away and when times get tough, you'll pull it out, and that tiny glimmer will represent hope for you and pride for all you have worked through.

I'm not going to sugarcoat this as you will still have so much you will have to work through and discover about yourself. In your forties all the paths you've taken, the self-disdain, the self-destruction will start to make sense to you. You will be diagnosed with bipolar disorder, and hand in hand with that will go ADHD. You'll see that you never were stupid or crazy as so many had told you. You will cry for days in relief.

There are so many other things that I can tell you about your life's journey, but you'll figure it all out. No, I will not say that it's all going to be better from there on out. There will be horrible lows and great accomplishments such as going back to school at almost the age of fifty and garnering your bachelor's degree in history. However, I will tell you that you will have to work steadily to make it through and not give up. One day you'll hear a song by The Indigo Girls and a particular lyric will stand out to you. You'll come to the understanding that it's easiest to allow the insatiable hunger of the darkness to overcome your very being, but it's hardest to try and climb out of that darkness in search of the light of self-love, and emotional well-being. This will be a fight that is constantly a part of your life. There will be times when your struggle will seem insurmountable, and it may take you a while to pull yourself out of it, but you must understand that plummeting into the dark is easy and yet emerging back into the light is hard.

I will leave you with something that I say to everyone, and you need to remember that no matter how bad you are, how good you are, how many mistakes you make, and no matter your accomplishments.........." But, I Love ya!"

Lindsey Warren

# DEAR TRAVIS,

Y ou're doing just fine. Keep being the quiet kid and folx will soon recognize you for the caring and funny kid that you are. Keep your family close. Hug your grandparents more often and call them as much as you can. Keep reading, writing, and running. All of those things will pay off later. They'll not leave you and will give you hope and solace at times when you feel like you need it.

Keep loving music too. That'll stay with you and be a balm during hard times as well. Know there's something different about you. It'll take a while (until college) but embrace it. It's ok. You're neither early nor late, but right on time. Keep developing your leadership skills because you'll need them later too. You'll find love and then lose it. It's one of the best/worst feelings you'll have, but you'll know that it's worth it all in the end. Keep your head up, eyes forward, and heart open.

Love,
Travis Rountree
    Author & Assistant Professor

# HEY GIRL!

Remember the day your seventh grade English teacher returned your short story assignment? You earned a C. She told you your grammar was exceptional and that you hit all the requirements, but she had a problem with the topic. You've always been a geek about space travel, ever since you watched Neil Armstrong walk on the moon, so you decided to write the story of an astronaut who crashed her ship and needed help to get home again. The astronaut was a feline-looking alien, from another galaxy, who was stuck on a moon similar to ours, and she used her cleverness and training to build herself an escape pod. Granted, at twelve years old, you didn't have much understanding of escape velocity or fuel usage in rockets, so the science was pretty skimpy. But the story wasn't about science — it was about not giving up in the face of danger, and of using ingenuity to make the best of a bad situation.

The teacher saw none of that. She told you there were no such things as aliens, and even if there were, women could never be astronauts because of their physical limitations. Besides, speculative fiction was not real writing. It was silly nonsense that adults learned to ignore, and you were too old by then to still be entertained by such childishness. She recommended you stick to writing only about what you know.

She was wrong.

You went on to write about eating watermelon in the summer and falling in love with boys who considered your body too ugly to be looked at, and loneliness. In your journal you wrote your thoughts about all the great fantasy and science fiction books you were reading, and how you wished you knew more about science and magic and such so that you, too, would be qualified to write stories like those people did. When no one was looking, you came up with little stories about leprechauns and unicorns and girls who used their robots to steal jewels from kings. Now and then you let trusted friends see your work, and they loved your stories. But you didn't trust their opinions – they were kids like you, so what did they know?

You were wrong.

Eventually, you went to college. The English department offered a short story writing class, and you wanted to sign up for it, but the description warned you that genre fiction (science fiction, fantasy, mystery, romance, and Western) was strictly forbidden. So you took Shakespeare and French Literature and Intro to Mythology and a bunch of other classes instead. You learned all sorts of interesting things and wrote those details into the stories you couldn't help crafting.

In your twenties, you decided to try submitting some of your short stories to magazines. You even sold a couple to small markets. You decided to try bigger ones. Fantasy & Science Fiction rejected your story as being too close to something they'd already bought. Talebones said another story was too bloody for them. And Asimov's told you the environmental horror tale you sent them was unbelievable since the climate would never change like that, and even if it did, it wouldn't be thanks to human interference. You stopped submitting, because those editors knew best, didn't they?

They were wrong.

Eventually, you joined a writing group and met a published author who took you by the hand and helped you see that writing was not out of your reach, that your stories were not ridiculous or incorrect, that you did have the ability to write work others would want to read. If it hadn't been for her, you might still be working in an industry that didn't fulfill you, with friends who didn't believe in you. She managed to convince you that all those people who insisted you stop were doing it for reasons that had nothing to do with you.

Now that you're sixty, you often look back with regret. Regrets over the limitation placed on your self-esteem, over not believing the friends who encouraged you, over assuming that you were wasting your time and energy, overthrowing away the stories you wrote in the days before word processors because you often wonder if they could have been workshopped and improved enough to sell. But regret doesn't put words on paper, and the past can't be repaired.

Instead, keep putting words on paper, so that when the last day finally arrives, you can look back and say, "Hey, I wasn't wrong after all."

Love,
Misty Massey
Author

# FILL THEM WITH LIFE

Sweet boy. You're only fourteen. Still hopeful. Still tender. Still unbruised.

You go down to the lake, sit on the dock, and look to the south where two enormous oaks frame the shore like curtains frame a stage. And you dream. You dream of bigger, better, faster, more. Of fame and fortune. Of beauty and bravery. Of glamour and gold.

And yet you're still not dreaming big enough for what life has in store.

Your world is smaller than you realize on that dirt road in Michigan. And there's so much beauty in that. Where you come from is going to mean things you can't comprehend. So try to appreciate it a little extra. It's shaping you. It's in your cells. It will always be a part of you. Even if you are not always a part of it.

Understand that things come in their time. You'll be impatient, but if you got everything you wanted when you wanted it, you might never have left the state. You might be happy in Ann Arbor all these years later (and all these years later, you still feel an acute yearning to be in Ann Arbor), but, trust, you will count your blessings you didn't find love or success there.

Because you are not Basic, you will be cast in the role of The Friend. This will devastate you for years (for good reason). It will suck. It will *suck*. But there is value to be found in being The Friend.

You will find your constitution and your voice by playing that character. As an observer you'll learn about human behavior—the foibles, the wisdoms, the weaknesses—as friends and strangers live out dramas you are not invited to be part of. Those lessons will fuel your writing. And they will give you the foundation to confidently take center stage when you (finally) become The Leading Man.

This means you will be a late bloomer. But rejoice in that. Because that means you do not peak in high school.

Nor in college.

As a matter of fact, you haven't peaked yet, as of this writing. (That's a good thing because you are still striding forward.)

Be patient with others, and yourself. (You'll struggle with this.)

Spite is great motivation, but don't let it motivate you. (You will struggle with this, too.)

Envy will attempt to derail you—and it will succeed at various turns (it is your biggest demon)—but, at all costs, don't compare yourself to others. (You still struggle with this.)

You will find that people are not gentle with your fragile heart. Some are mindless, some are lost and grappling with their own insecurities and doubts, and many are straight-up assholes. These groups include some of your best friends, friends you think are soul mates, friends who stencil tattoos on your life, friends who are part of your fabric. They will abandon you for reasons you will never understand. The plot twists will leave you breathless. You will be devastated. You will crack. You will shatter. Don't let that taint the memories of your friendships. (You haven't mastered that yet. And you might never.)

Those scars will mold you, and they will cover up—messily, hideously—those tattoos. But, in the end, those experiences will also inform your writing, your understanding of relationships, and your insight into the disarray of humanity. Even so, you will wonder if the implosion of your heart was worth it. You will never know the answer to that.

You've just started writing. Keep at it. It is how you will make sense of the world, how you will process the amusement park madness of life. You'll strive to teach others the lessons you've learned with your works. Whether they learn from them or not is out of your control.

Most people do nothing but run down the clock. They aspire to nothing more than the next binge-worthy television show. The newest scandal. The latest fast-food sensation.

You are not those people. You will fill your days with aspirations, goals, and dreams. That doesn't mean you can while those days away, your head in the clouds. You get where you get because you take action. Even now you are spinning countless plates trying to make shit happen. Some of those plates will fall. But many of them will remain in the air, spinning like the top at the end of "Inception." (You'll get that reference in a couple of decades.)

It will be hard to remember at your lowest moments, but things do get better.

Then they get worse.

Then they get better.

Then they get worse.

Then they get better.

That is a truth you will dispense to a twelve-year-old girl on a rooftop party in downtown LA many years from now (it takes many of those years to learn it, if one ever truly does) when she confides in you how horrid middle school is (you remember that well). You will hearten her. And armor her. Your wisdom will guide her. And if you can gain the trust of a child, you're doing something right.

Now, you live in Hollywood. You've written a successful novel (that sprang from the glistening shards of your shattered heart). You get fan letters! You have a handsome, Emmy-winning partner of twenty years. You've walked red carpets. You've been to movie premieres and the Grammys.

You've traveled to countless countries, gambling in a Monacan casino and partying in an Italian castle. New York. London. Paris. Rome. Cabo. San Francisco. Amsterdam. Vegas. Berlin. You've painted them all red. (You're still working on Asia and Africa, but you'll get there.) You've won a screenwriting contest. You have written nine feature scripts and are pitching them to producers and managers. You have been the managing editor of two national magazines and editor-in-chief of another. You are a theater critic for Broadway World and a member of the Los Angeles Drama Critics Circle.

You are in Mensa. You've DONE SHIT.

This isn't intended to be masturbatory (I know you're blushing right now at that word), it's intended to buoy you so that you persevere with confidence and pluck, treat yourself with kindness and empathy, and continue to dream bigger. Because, while you do leave behind that dirt road, it's a circuitous odyssey, filled with hardships and heartbreak, joys and jubilations, thistles, switchbacks, valleys and plateaus. Try to stay the course with a steady hand and a steadier heart. Embrace the zigs and the zags.

You're not there yet, where you want to be, but you've gotten so much more than you allowed yourself to dream of sitting on that dock. Now you look at a pair of palm trees framing your horizon like a stage. It's different from how it was back on that lake in Michigan. But it's also the same. And, for as much as you've changed (and you've changed dramatically, in ways you would never believe), you are also the same fourteen-year-old boy at heart. You're still manifesting bigger, better, faster, more.

You still dream.

The days will go fast whether you fill them with life or run down the clock.

So, fill them with life.
See you soon,

Harker Jones
Author and former Editor in Chief of Out magazine

# HEY, SUGA!

I know you're probably wondering who the heck sent you this letter and you're likely going straight to the end of it to see who it's from.

Now you're wondering why the letter is signed with your name. You're also probably really impressed that your name is spelled correctly.

This is weird, huh? Well, it's going to get much weirder, so go grab a mirror and find a comfortable place to sit because it's story time!

Now let me start by telling you who I am and why I'm writing...

I am the forty-seven-year-old you. Yes, Suga, I said forty-seven! Don't freak out, it only seems old because you're only ten and Momma just turned thirty-one. If it makes you feel any better, honey you look fabulous at forty-seven!

I'm writing to let you know about a very special gift you are going to receive when you get older.

I know you have the attention span of a goldfish (don't worry, most of the population will be on medication for that in fifteen to twenty years) but try to stay focused.

Did you grab that mirror? I'll wait…

- Take a good look at yourself in that mirror and let me tell you a few things you need to know about the person looking back at you.
- You were hand-crafted by God, so embrace those things that you feel are different.
- God made you different because of the purpose He has for you. You have no idea what that is at your age but trust me.
- You may have already noticed that all types of people are drawn to you. Just keep being who you are because you are already operating in your purpose.

Now let's talk about that Ken doll that Momma won't buy for you.

- You're creative and just like the women raising you, you've learned to make what you have work for what you need.
- That desire to just transform your extra Barbie into a boy…GO WITH IT!
- Oh, by the way, Barbie's boobies are made of hard plastic and those Fiskars scissors are only going to scrape off her tan.
- Also, you don't have to cut all her hair off unless you just want to. The hair length doesn't make your doll any more or less a boy.

- You have no idea right now how this foreshadows what's to come in your life.
- Lemonade, Knock Outs, and Homeruns
- You're so young and life has already tried to beat the hell out of you. What can I say? Life is hard sometimes and that will continue to be the case as you grow.
- You will grow up hearing people say things like, "When life gives you lemons, make lemonade."
- I'm here to tell you that life will throw all kinds of shit at you (lemons included), but life isn't going to give you shit!
- Don't worry, sweetheart, you have served up some of the sweetest lemonade. You have taken a few punches but ultimately knocked out your opponents. And those curveballs…girl, you have not only hit some home runs, but you have knocked them out of the park.
- Everything life throws at you is molding you into the perfect person to receive your special gift so keep pushing and don't give up.

Rainbows

- There's just something about rainbows that you love.
- Rainbows will eventually become the symbol of a very special community that is filled with the most amazing people.
- The people in this community are often overlooked, misunderstood, and mistreated because of their uniqueness.

- You will be known as an ally to this
community long before your special gift arrives.
Okay, so now let's get to your special gift!!

I hope you're still sitting down in a comfortable spot, and I really hope you're not still staring at yourself in that mirror. Put the mirror down and focus, Suga!

You will marry the most amazing man that God created just for you. This one comes after your first husband but being married to the first one is important because it teaches you a lot of things, and there is a gift at the end of that one too. When you're twenty-nine, you will find you are expecting your third child. Yes, three…don't worry, the other two are equally amazing. You think you want another little boy, but the doctor tells you the baby is a girl.

Just before you turn thirty, your gift arrives. She is the most beautiful baby girl with the most beautiful hair. You realize immediately that it didn't really matter if you had a boy or a girl. You instantly fall in love with your baby and from that moment, you want to do everything you can to be the best possible mom for that baby.

Your baby girl will start to grow up and develop her own little personality and style. You will notice that your little girl would rather be in pants and shorts instead of dresses. That's not a big deal because you hated it when Momma put those frilly dresses on you. You will dress her in what makes her most comfortable because you're her mommy and mommy will always love and support her.

Your baby girl likes playing with toy trucks, cars, tools, her brother's wrestlers, etc. Your Momma will fuss at you for buying her the toys she likes, but Momma will always find something to fuss about. You will buy your little girl the toys she likes and tell her about the little girl you met in elementary school who liked the same kind of toys. You will encourage her to play with the toys she likes and to be unapologetically who she is. You will let her know that you're her mommy and mommy will always love and support her.

One day on your day off from work, you will take her by your office to meet your friends. On that day you will introduce her to Miss Jesse. When you return to the car to go home, she will tell you how much fun she had and how much she loves your friend, Miss Jesse. You will then be asked why you called Miss Jesse a "Miss" and if you noticed that Miss Jesse is a boy. Remember the rainbows and that community of amazing people I told you about? Miss Jesse is one of those amazing people.

You will tell your baby that you noticed and ask her to close her eyes. You then tell her to imagine getting all dressed up in her favorite clothes with her hair done up in her favorite style. You will tell her to think about how beautiful she looks. When you see her smiling because she can imagine it, you tell her to walk to the mirror, open her eyes, and imagine seeing a boy standing in the mirror instead of the beautiful face she imagined. You will then explain that's how Miss Jesse feels every day. She doesn't feel like a boy, she just has a boy body. You will go on to say you are Miss Jesse's friend, and no matter what body she is in, you will always love and support her.

Your little girl will become a teenager and want to shave her head. Remember what I told you about the Barbie doll?

It's just hair and doesn't change who you are. So, you will grab the clippers and shave her head. You're her mommy and you will always love and support her.

While you're cooking dinner one night, your little girl (who's not so little anymore) will tell you that she likes girls. You will say, "OK" and ask if she wants any more broccoli. You will let her know that you're her mommy and you will always love and support her.

A few months later, your little girl will tell you that she's "Bi". That means she likes boys and girls. You will say, "OK" and you will let her know that you're her mommy and you will always love and support her.

Another few months will pass, and your little girl will tell you that she's Transgender and tell you to use the pronouns he/him. You will ask questions and you will let him know that he's been your "little girl" for sixteen years, so it may be a challenge, but you will try. You will also let him know that you are going to mess up and ask that he give you grace and mercy as you navigate this journey together. You will then let him know that you are his mommy, and you will always love and support him.

You will ask him if it's okay to reach out to a couple of your Transgender friends to help you find your way. He will give you the okay and you will reach out to Miss Jesse first amongst a few other friends because you do not want to mess this up. Your community of friends are going to be such a blessing to you. They will guide you, cheer for you, comfort you, and pray for you.

This is not going to be an easy road and there will be a lot of adjustments. You will be helping your son navigate this life while you and your husband are trying to find your way at the same time. Here's an example of some of the things you will feel in a really short period of time.

- **Shock** – because you knew he was different, but you didn't know he was a boy.
- **Acceptance** – because once you laid eyes on your baby, it didn't matter what gender the baby was. You are his mommy, and you will always love and support him.
- **Fear** – now you have another black son to worry about being killed because he's black and male. On top of that, he's Transgender which places him in even more danger of being hurt or killed.
- **Greif** – even though your child is still alive, you mourn the loss of the daughter you had for sixteen years.
- **Confusion** – You no longer have your daughter, but her body is still alive hugging and kissing you goodnight, eating dinner with you, greeting you at the door when you get home from work.
- **More Confusion** – When your son decides to put a dress on your daughter's body and for a brief moment you forget that she's now a boy.
- **More Greif** – When you've had that brief moment with your daughter only to say goodbye to her again.
- **Stress** – Your son goes through a period of being suicidal and you have to find help fast.

- **Relief** – When the suicidal period is over and you're just happy to have your child back no matter what body he's in or what gender he identifies as.
- **More Stress** – On your marriage and your spouse because everyone is at a different place in this journey.
- **Unsure** – How do we tell people? Who should tell them?
- **Confrontational** – What if somebody says something mean to or about our baby? Your claws are out and ready to protect your child.
- **Assured** – When you remember that God chose you to be this child's mother. You were hand-crafted by God and equipped with whatever is needed to raise this special gift from God.
- **Joy** – when life just feels normal.
- **Blessed** – When your beautiful son hugs you, tells you that he loves you, and tells you that you are a great mother.
- **Inspired** – To be a mother figure, auntie, or big sister to any child in the community whose parents have turned them away.
- **Proud** – To have been given the opportunity to be his mom.

Oh, sweet girl, you have so much to look forward to in this life and even more to be thankful for. Your son wants you to know that "you're doing a great job, kid. Keep up the good work, and I love you."

I'm not going to take up any more of your time because you have a beautiful life to go live. I love you, Suga. You keep being you and everything will be alright.

Love Always,
Jojuan Gallman
Mother

# A LETTER TO MY
# FORMER SELF

Hey! Yeah, it's weird getting a letter from yourself from the future, but let's be honest, you're not really surprised this is a thing, right? That's what I thought.

You're wondering what I'm doing this for...Well, I thought maybe you could use it. You're dealing with a lot right now, figuring out who you are and all. Just know, all that drama going on won't be there later in life. Oh, and you're WAY better off without that cheating bastard in your life. Seriously...you've dodged a bullet (2Doggz even says so years later). So let go of that fear and hate, carrying it around won't serve you well. I know it'll be hard to do but try.

Right now, you're contemplating not going back to teaching and moving to New York City to do theater. DO IT! It's the right call. It is so stressful, but this move is only #2 of more in your life and by doing this you'll have the courage later in life to move on and know how to do so successfully. Your friends in SC will always be in your life. They are an amazing support system, and you'll miss them like a limb, but you need to branch out to find you. Years later they'll still be there for you. Bonds like that last. But do yourself one big favor, in 2020 you'll have some serious time on your hands…call Joe and be there for him. You don't get friends in your life for as long as you assume.

Lastly, not all of those who appear to be friends are. You'll notice once you are not in the position to cast them in shows, they may not stick around. It's okay, you'll start writing again and meet a group of people who will remind you of your SC crew. You'll find your place amongst them and write some fun books. Yes, books! You! Imagine that!

I'll let you get back to your world…go pack for NYC and take that leap. You'll never regret it, and it helps build you into who you are meant to be. And when you see the SC gang again, hug them all hard and let them know you love them.

Oh…I know you're not one to invest but you should do so in Apple and Facebook. Trust me.

Love, *Your Future Self* xoxo
Tamsin L. Silver
Author

P.S. Your weight is going to go up again and down a few times…it's okay. Learn to love you in any shape! I'm trying to do that now but if you could start earlier on that, it'll help a lot. Life is more than weight. It's the people in your life. Love them and do all the things!

******This letter is in loving memory of Joe Gann******

# TO MY YOUNGEST SELVES,

First of all, I am proud of you. The many things you endured and survived, looking back, seem endless. But for the most part, you just shouldered though. The physical injuries, soul-crushing job, the sea of hate that has been so much of this society, all failed to defeat you.

I am proud that you did not let society change you. The Bookworm, the kid who cared too much, the young man who never strove to be popular by doing the things that would have led to that path, as those things did not resonate with who you were.

Proud of you for all those you took under your wing, the schoolmates, social oddballs from everywhere, the comic shop, the fish club, even the mundanes at work. So few people have someone step up for them, for no other reason than that they needed someone.

Not everything works out, the injuries from the car wreck will be a daily struggle for the rest of your life. A stable romantic relationship just does not happen. And while society advances, evil is always there, sometimes seemingly unchecked. But prevail!

To my youngest selves, the Internet is going to be a life changer. Contact with like-minded folks all over the world. It will change your life in so many ways. People whom you would only imagine even meeting will become the people who you communicate with often, to the point that they are your friends.

And one day, you will come out. Your family and friends will know and not care. And while it still is not totally safe, the vast majority of people who know you will be there to love you as you are.

And that totally out of whack-giving thing you do? Oh, younger selves, the things that leads to.

You are literally going to become Santa Claus. What you do will be made into a verb! Book Santa is but one of many titles bestowed upon you.

The people you will meet, both far spread and close to home, will both enrich and support you, in so many mind-blowing ways.

I think very few people get the life they expect. I know I did not. But the life I have had and hope to have has been amazing.

Hold on, be strong, and know, I am so proud of you.

Dino Hicks

Patron Saint of Indie Authors, Book Santa, Muddy Monter, Dino the Dinosaur, Bookworm, The Warped Avenger, Hippy Santa and Dino Claus and the Labradorite Fairy, by these names, you shall know him.

# ONE BETTER

It's not the things we believe to be false, but rather the things we know to be true that are often the hardest pills to swallow. These truths are the voices which whisper in your ear, the ones which cause that sinking feeling in the pit of your stomach. You know the one. They are the things which leave you feeling stiff, frozen, weak, unable to speak, frozen in place.

Now, close your eyes. Imagine yourself standing on a boat, a dinghy if you will. You are out in the middle of the ocean. Storm clouds completely surround you, yet at the same time, the water remains completely still—a mockery of your feelings as the surface appears flat and emotionless.

Your boat sits in the eye of a hurricane, providing you a momentary respite from the trials and tribulations of your past. Soon, a light breeze wafts by, followed by another, then another, each one stronger than the last. Now, open your eyes, and steel your resolve. Your renewed confidence is going to be your greatest defense as you prepare to face the challenges of the storm's oncoming onslaught.

Storms suck. And I'm not just referencing the ones framed in an eloquently worded analogy about the weather. The worst storms don't even involve a single drop of rain. Instead, great turbulences are formed when the skewed perspective of one's moral compass comes into play. When large groups of these people gather, the ensuing chaos can be overwhelming. If these groups contain members of your own family, the people who should be supporting you the most, it can be especially heartbreaking.

I understand how you feel when the people who have offended you don't even realize that they have done it. You know what I say to that. Screw them. Don't listen to them, put those voices on mute. Chin up, Buttercup. The people who are against you might be rocking the boat. But you're the one driving it. Whatever you're going through now might seem hard, but you'll make it through to the end stronger. You're still standing, because at the end of the day, you have weathered the storm, and have come out the other end one better.

Rey Nichols
Author of Until Death – An Eric Kent Investigation: Case 1 published by Gold Dust Publishing, and the Apollo Grant series published by Mocha Memoir Press.

# TO MY DEAR ONE,

The other morning, I woke up hours before my alarm, as I am wont to do. As I lay in bed, the stillness of the early morning hour was interrupted by a sudden flash of déjà-vu. As an avowed back sleeper for the past several years, the peculiar position of my body at that moment (on my side, with my knees curled up and arms curled in) is a position in which I haven't laid in quite some time. The shock of finding myself in this position again after so many years was like a kind of key, which opened a door to my past. A door that connected me to a time where I lay like that every night not wrapped in a sense of comfort and safety, which is what I feel now, but in fear and loathing. A desire to shrink into nothingness. Through the threshold, I see him weeping. And to that boy, my dearest of dear ones, I extend my hand through the door with a veritable cascade of love propelling me forward.

My dear one, I am sorry for what you endure.

I am sorry that you must witness your mother slowly slip

away from you into the choking miasma of addiction. My heart is heavy for you because I know that the one person you need – the one person you believe will hold your hand and guide you as you stumble into the heart of your truth and what it means for you – will be the one person whose love is conditional, balancing on the axis of how authentically you live said truth in relation to her ravenous and insatiable need for control. I know how trying to appease her and keep her close while navigating the complexities of your blossoming sexuality will take its toll on you, both mentally and physically. I remember how it led you to run into the arms of grown men who seemed to accept and love you on the surface but were instead taking predatory advantage of your teenaged vulnerability. I know intimately how it caused you to indulge in substances and behaviors that nearly cost you the fire you were fighting so hard to keep burning. And I still feel the echoes of the self-disgust that courses through your veins deep inside my bone marrow today. Please know that while the guilt and grief over what you say and do to survive hangs heavy around your neck now, you will be free from the albatross someday. You do what you need to greet the next morning, with the tools you have at your disposal. Give yourself space and grace.

My dear one, I am sorry for what you hear.

Hearing your mother tell her friend on the phone that she views you as a "challenge from God" cuts deep. Enduring your teachers' daily Bible devotionals, almost all of which end with them telling you that you are going to burn in Hell simply for being who you are is like a routine whip to the face. Listening to the first boy you love tell his friends that he thinks you're nothing more than a toy to be used and discarded burns hotter in your heart than a thousand dying stars. Eavesdropping on your classmates' parent's gossip about how big of a failure you'll be as an adult to build up their own children and spite your mother is like a knife to the gut. While what your mother says will, unfortunately, stay with you, the scar becomes less and less noticeable with each passing season. And the other comments, dear one, fade and become wordless reverberations in the halls of your history. The dulled, chipped, and rusted blades of their words become impotent as you tend to your light and stand firmly within it. There will even come a time when their names are largely lost to you, which will be the true testament of your transcendence.

My dear one, I am sorry for what you believe.

I know that it is hard not to internalize and believe every sharp word you hear, coming at you from all sides. Contrary to how you read and interpret the Bible in your own time, you defer to your teachers' image of a vengeful, hateful God who wants you dead for no other reason than for being yourself. You accept that your mother has your best interest at heart when she wakes you up in the middle of the night to drip "holy water" on your head as you sleep to exorcise the "gay demon" from your soul. When your reflection tells you every morning that you're undeserving of true love and will end up dying alone, you drink in his words like a heady elixir. This toxic chorus of voices is charismatic and compelling, so it is easy to fall prey to their words and feed the beast. But know that while you come dangerously close to the precipice of true despair, you will purge their poison before succumbing to it. The path and process of this detoxification has yet to appear before you, but you will know when the time comes.

In the end, my dear one, I offer you hope.

The hardest thing for you to conjure right now is a desire to see the next sunrise. I know that you currently pray for death every night and I still have the scar on my right wrist from your attempt to hasten her arrival. But I stand before you as proof positive that there *is* a future for you, shuddering with anticipation to unfold. While you want nothing more than simplicity, especially because you live in such chaos, the road you are to take is long, winding, and riddled with pitfalls and detours. You will lose many people along the way, including your mother, but you will become stronger, more confident, and more self-assured. The ember of a dream to which you secretly tend every night will grow into a flame, and you will carry that flame through years and across time until you release it to the Universe on your first night in Japan. And in that moment, as you stand on your balcony and look up at the stars while the flame rises ever upward, you will finally know what it's like to feel pride in your accomplishments.

Wipe those tears. Stretch out your legs. And break free from that pose of self-pity and self-doubt. Stand firm in your strength and resilience. And know that, across time and space, your older self-watches over you, prouder than anyone has ever been.

Mitchell Kissack
Assistant Language Teacher (Japan)

# HEY KIDDO,

As I write this I am, you are, we are… forty-six years old. There is so much I'd like to tell you about our life, but I don't want to spoil all the surprises.

Around now you are eighteen years old, having the time of your life with the friends you've made at Jutenhoops. I'm happy to tell you that quite a few of them are still in our life today! Actually, most all of your lifelong friends are still in your life today. I'm very proud of you for making sure those connections were never lost. Time and distance, as you know, has a way of fading friendships as we grow up. I will tell you that a good amount of them come back into your life when you're an adult. No, you're not an adult now, trust me. You won't though. You learn lessons your way. That is usually the hard way, and we still do it on occasion even now.

But maybe if the advice comes from your older self, it'll resonate more? Maybe it'll mean more? Maybe you'll trust it more? I hope…

Quit diminishing yourself to fit into a space not meant for you. That includes romantic relationships, friendships, jobs, etc. Especially romantic relationships. That one bears repeating. I don't mind ruining this surprise – but that will NEVER, EVER work out the way you want it to. And you will get your heart broken every single time. Along that vein, quit ignoring the people who love how bold, brassy, wild, and unabashed you are. These are the gems, baby girl. These are the ones who love you for YOU. These are the ones who deserve your time, your attention, and your heart.

That being said, I want you to practice pausing. Pause before you react. I mean this, Carrie. Take a moment or two, or ten before you react. Count if you have to. Flying off the handle in a nanosecond rarely works in our favor. I will tell you that we do come to realize that reactions come from one of two places – from our ego, or from our soul. And our ego has cost us some very dear people in our lives. It's what has FORCED us to stop and figure out why. It's made us realize that behaving from our soul is the much calmer route. In everything we do. In every choice we make. And it NEVER steers us wrong. So, learn to pause. To take a breath. I'm not saying the choices will always be easy, but when they're made from our soul, we never regret them. Believe me when I say, we have regretted quite a bit of things because our ego loves to shout. Need to learn how to sit that girl down and make her be silent more often than not. Start now.

I know you miss her every day, so I'm happy to tell you Jennifer is still in your life. Every day. This very month of this letter you two have been best friends for thirty-eight years. Every life event, big or small, you two have been there for each other. Your roads have diverged, but never far apart. They are always close enough for one of you to pop over and walk beside the other when needed. And we're getting to an age now where that's needed quite a bit. In all the good and bad ways. By the grace of God, you two are paired for life. And yeah, we still laugh as much as we always did! Case in point, she just texted me the best photo and caption ever, assuring me we're still living our best lives as she bought a case of protein drinks. You'll find out what texting is soon enough. And protein drinks too, for that matter. Hahaha!

Be sure to hug your family more often. By now we've lost a lot of them. Most of them. I will tell you that you have a son, and yes, you named him that name we chose in the eighth grade – Coy James. He's the most beautiful, wonderful, gentle, hysterical, kind, and amazing soul that God ever put on this earth.

There are going to be so many bumps in the road. And quite a few ditches. Financial ones. Motherhood ones. Romantic ones. Family ones. But you get through it. You're very much your mother's daughter. You never give up. You always do what you have to do to keep moving forward and get through it.

And I know it's a true fear of yours, so I'm glad to tell you, yes, Mom is still here. And she's the most annoying grandparent EVER. She worships Coy and now I finally see how our relationship with Grandma always annoyed her. Coy can do no wrong in her eyes. He is the golden child. It's okay, our time of being a grandparent will come. And they will rue the day.

Listen to your intuition more often. I promise you; it will change and guide your whole life when you're my age.

Trust Josh a little bit more. He's a cool guy, one that deserves your time, your attention, and your heart. Don't think he's always bull-shitting you. I promise that one turns out pretty cool.

I'm very proud of you. You've really done well in life. I've never once been embarrassed of you, never wanted to change you. Tweak some things, yes. But never change you. If I could go back and see you right now, I'd hug you so tight. I'd tell you, you are never alone. I'd tell you one day you're gonna wish you were as fat as you think you are now. And that no, we never lose those curls. Sorry. Hahaha!
I love you, kiddo. See you in the mirror.

Love,

You

Carrie Hopper
Podcast cohost History of a Haunting

# NOTE TO SELF,

I miss me terribly. This is what we will call a tragedy. The story of you is this tragedy of a life full of potential wasted. A life's spent waiting, waiting for something. Something that never arrived, and when it did it never was as big as you'd expected.

That girl at the front of the room ACTUALLY did notice you. You just intimidated her with the image you put up to keep everyone from noticing how weak you really felt. How small you thought you were.

It seemed life would fade away, drifting further every day into the dirty magic you let others play on you. But when they left you drained and alone in a room... you rose up to scream in the face of the silence that beckoned you. The silence that waited for you all dressed up in roses offering a dream.

You saw through the lies. After years of marching to someone else's beat, you discovered your own voice. While your guitar made you weep. And your words ran from your veins across your pages. You'll meet and lose muses and angels will call your name and fly away just out of reach.

One day, A Restless Angel Claimed Her Eternal Love, but that story ended in blood, as every good true love story SHOULD end. There can never be a good ENDING to a story that isn't "Happily Ever After'. This too you'll overcome and although it will haunt you for a long time, you'll receive the greatest joy of your life. You'll find the one that replaces her will give you a son.

That story too will have an unhappy end but, the worse is yet to come. Hang in there. You'll see more happiness than pain.

There's joy to come and heartbreak. Some of that heartbreak will be of your own doing. Some angels will return to your life, for a little while and some will become your best friends, which will cause its own issues.

A little bit of a storybook will play out for you for a while, but that story will see muses become angels and your heartache become someone else's mirth. You'll be broken body and soul. You'll be broken for a while. It will hurt more than anything else ever had, but you'll be fixed by someone as broken as you.

You'll find yourself on a swinging bench drinking a cup of coffee. In this odd place You'll find someone who needs to heal themselves but will end up healing you. What was meant to be the end of your story will become another new beginning. A better life. Now you just have to stay the way.

You have to keep walking this broken road. I don't know how it will all end up, but I know that it will all be worth it. There is a beauty for your ashes... just hang in there.

We still have more pages to write. Though it may seem trite. IT DOES GET BETTER.

Eventually, their words leave your head, and you pull all those knives out of your heart. You find a better life. No, you do. Believe me. You find peace, you find yourself. You realize you were always good enough. You were always smart enough. You were always enough. Eventually, you find out that you are good enough for yourself. You find happiness alone. You find yourself and you're a better person than anyone, including you, thought you were.

Harry Mora
Author

# my past...

The things we learn as we grow are amazing. Unfortunately, we base our decisions on what people tell us and not what we think or feel. The reason is simple, we do not have the knowledge nor the experience to make a life-changing decision without talking to someone about our future. Typically, we talk to our friends who are the same age as us and who do not have the knowledge or the experience either. We may turn to our parents, but do they have the knowledge in the field you are looking to go into? As an example, I was offered an opportunity with a computer chip company, which we will talk about more later. I spoke to my dad, and he told me I was nuts. I didn't talk to the right people when opportunities hit me in the face growing up and to this day, I regret not taking those chances.

Cellphones

In 1989 I was told to buy stock in cell phones. I laughed and stated, "Besides me, who wants to walk around with a bag phone on their hip"? The salesman laughed and told me, "Everyone will have cell phones by the year 2000". I laughed at him. He begged me to invest just $100.00 a month, and if I couldn't afford that, invest what I could but INVEST. I never did and look at where cellphones are now. Look at who has cell phones now, everyone. I sure missed an opportunity. I closed that door because I listened to my family and friends. Outside of the salesman, not one person told me to invest in cell phones. Actually, most of them laughed at me because I was walking around with a bag phone over my shoulder. They said I looked like an idiot. I listened to the wrong people. I should have listened to the person who had knowledge of the industry, not people around me who knew nothing.

## Property For Sale

Shortly after turning down the cell phone opportunity, I found a house for sale with six-plus acres. The house needed some work, probably more than I could handle by myself. The house had potential, yes. But more importantly, the *property* had potential. Rumor had it, that area was the next part of town to be developed into housing developments. Long story short, everyone told me it was a long shot, it was more work than I could handle, and the wife was not happy with the house. She didn't care that the property had potential, she did not want to buy the home. The home and property was purchased about two months later. The person who purchased it sold it approximately a year later for 1.3 million. He made a mint off the home. Again, I lost out.

## Computer Chips

In 1990 I met a gentleman who started a computer chip

company. In June of 1991, he offered me to come work for his company - employee number 3. My wife and I just had our son in May so me starting a new job was totally out of the question. It did not matter what the guy offered me, or what his vision was, the wife was totally against it. The gentleman had a vision like I had never seen before. I knew he was going somewhere. Three years later he sold his company for 3 million dollars.

Restaurant Business

Every Sunday we went to a specific restaurant for dinner. We got to know the owner very well, first name basis. He told us he was moving the restaurant to a larger location and wanted me to come work for him. Do I need to say, the wife was not a big fan of me leaving a stable job for a new job? About a year later, business was booming, he approached me about taking his business to a franchise level. Again, I had to turn him down. Today, he has eighteen franchisees, and he is retired at the beach.

All four of these situations have the same thing in common, I listened to the people around me, with the same knowledge and experience that I had. I did not talk to people who had true knowledge of these businesses or situations. Imagine where I could be if I had spoken to someone with me knowledge than myself. I know I think about it often. The lesson is very simple, never close a door until you do ALL the research you can, by yourself, with friends and family, and most importantly with people who have experience in the situation. Never be afraid to ask for guidance.

With all that said, in 2014 a door opened, and I did not close it. At the age of forty-nine, I left a fourteen-year career to start my own business. Doing so, I lost my wife and kids.

It was going to happen anyway; I just made it happen sooner. I did the research about the franchise by myself. I asked my family about it, and only my daughter told me to go for it. I spoke to my friends and only one of them told me to go for it. I turned to the people in the industry. I showed them my research, my numbers, and my projections for a brand-new franchise. They all told me to jump on it. It's a chance of a lifetime, and it was, I went from working sixty-five plus hours a week, never having time off, being overweight, and tired all the time, to working forty-five hours a week, having more time off than I have ever had, I lost sixty pounds and I had more energy than when I was in my twenties. It was the best thing I ever did. As a matter of fact, the franchise was ranked in the top three in the United States in 2019. I made the right decision by not closing the door.

The franchise led me to start my own liquor business at the age of fifty-five. Crazy, right!! Opening the franchise gave me enough confidence to do the Vodka business and not even hesitate. Regardless of everyone telling me not to do it, AGAIN, I went with my research and the opinions of the people in the business, not my friends and family. Pulse Vodka is winning all sorts of awards for the blind tastings with the hagiarchies. Pulse Vodka will be a top Vodka in the next three years.

Your takeaway from this should be very simple. Believe in yourself, do your research, talk to the people who have the knowledge, and don't ask people on the same level as you and you will always make the right decision.

George Gerdes
One Community One Pulse
Owner, Pulse Vodka
Semper FI

# DEAR TEN-YEAR-OLD ME,

It's me – well, you – from eighteen years in the future. As surprised as you might be, you are still alive, and dare I say it, you are happy!

There is so much that I could say to you right now, but if I tried to say it all, I would never stop writing this letter to you.

So, instead, I'll focus on what I think needs to be said the most.

I can remember like it was yesterday how it feels to be where you are right now – uncertain, lonely, scared, guilty, ashamed. I know you lay awake at night, praying to God that you could just be normal. You don't know what's wrong with you, you don't know what it is that makes you different from everyone else, but you just want to be normal. You are tired of feeling like you can't exist in your body; you are exhausted from wishing with all your might that you could be as small as possible, invisible.

You don't know what's going on within you. You don't know why you always want to play male characters, why you always feel averse to pretending to be princesses or queens or witches. You don't know why at the sleepover of twenty girls who were dressing up as female pop stars and singing their hearts out, you dressed up as Tarzan and refused to be referred to as anything other than a man. You don't know why you insist on wearing shirts that are too big for you, or why when your best friend's sister talks about periods and you becoming a woman, you feel dizzy and out of breath. You don't share in the excitement your friends have about developing curves and going through puberty; while they discuss the growth of breasts and hips, you try to push the panic down and down and down until you barely feel anything at all. You aren't sure why, when going clothes shopping, you are drawn to the men's section immediately.

All you really know is that every time you look up homosexuality in the Bible, your heart breaks just a little bit more. Every time you are excluded from male activities, you feel a little bit more alone. Every time Mom brings home another feminine shirt that is pink and glittery and tells you to get rid of the masculine oversized t-shirts you have, you feel more and more unseen. Every time you compare yourself to the girls in your class, you don't understand why it's so hard for you to be like them. When you look at the boys, you don't understand why you *can't* be like them. All you really know is that it always feels like there is a distance between you and everyone else, and you don't know why...so, you've convinced yourself that there must be something wrong with you.

One day, you saw a magazine in the line at the grocery store covering the breaking news of Chaz Bono, Sonny & Cher's transgender son. You never even knew it was possible to change your gender – you had never heard the term "transgender" – but as you flipped through the pages and looked at the photos of Chaz confidently walking down the street as himself, you didn't feel disgust for him the way those around you did. While everyone was calling him a lesbian, you thought about how ridiculous that was. He couldn't be a lesbian – he was a man. Suddenly, something made sense to you, but it was impossible to articulate what it was that made sense. All you knew was that your shoulders relaxed, your brain grew quiet, and the constant knot in your stomach began to ease. You suddenly didn't feel quite so alone. You felt awestruck, you felt happy for him. You had never felt so seen in your life, even if you didn't have the words to explain where this feeling was coming from or why.

Your mother told you to stop reading that magazine and to put it back, and you filed her discomfort at a transgender man's existence into your brain for later reference – twelve years in the future, you will remember this moment and you will become sick to your stomach as you imagine that disgust directed at you.

You're just ten years old right now, trying to figure everything out, and it's scary to feel so alone and confused with nobody to talk to. As you grow, you will continue to face challenges and obstacles. You will have struggles with depression and anxiety – different kinds than those around you. You will have a hard time connecting with friends as you start to develop feelings for your friends who are girls and jealousy of your friends who are boys. As school dances approach, you will be filled with anxiety and shame, and you will spend the night before trying not to fake an illness to get out of going. Every day you will look at the spread of makeup you have been told you should use, and every day, through clenched jaws, you will decide not to use it. You will be told by male classmates that you should wear tighter clothing to show off your feminine figure, and because you just want to be like everyone else, you will do so. And every time you do so, you will wish you didn't exist.

You will dedicate all your time and energy to being perfect at everything for your family – straight A's, well-behaved, excelling in all that you do. You will frame this as making up for who you are – someone that nobody could ever actually love.

And, in the meantime, you will be hurting, confused, and angry. You will turn to cutting and other self-harming behaviors. Suicide will, unfortunately, be on your mind. And you will start to invest yourself in things like drugs and alcohol because existing under those conditions is easier than when you're sober. You will drive to school in the morning after drinking a beer, and you will go into Physics class with a bottle full of Mountain Dew and wine.

I wish with all of my heart that I could go back in time and tell you not to do these things – that I could provide you with the clarity, love, and acceptance that you so desperately need. You are only a kid, and life is so trying for you already. You deserve to have someone fighting for you.

I want to tell you that, despite the struggles of growing up in the closet as a queer and trans kid, despite the challenges you will face as you grow and explore your identity, you will be okay. Honestly, you will be better than okay.

As a kid, you always fight for the underdog because you know what it's like to have nobody in your corner. As an adult, you will fight just as fiercely for those who do not have the privilege to do so. You have a purpose, and you are so brave for hanging on when everything feels like you should let go.

When you decide to transition at twenty-two-years-old, everything will start to fall into place. Everything will make sense as your body begins to reflect your mind. The feeling you will have when you grow a beard, get top surgery, and experience the euphoria of being called a man in public will make up for all of the struggles – all of the difficulties will have been worth it. You will be so thankful when you look in the mirror and see your true self reflected, that you didn't give up.

So, on the days when you feel like nothing will get better, that you will always hold these heavy, deep-rooted emotions of shame and guilt and fear, that you will always be invisible and on your own, please know that this is temporary. Please know that you're a boy now even if you don't have the words to express that, even if you don't know what that really means yet, and one day you will become a man, and you will be able to be all the things you never could be when you were younger.

Transitioning won't be easy – it is a complicated process

that is full of adjustments, changes, and difficulties. But every single change, every single difficulty, is worth the outcome that saves your life. The first choice you make for yourself is to stay alive, and I'm happy to report that you will feel so proud of yourself for putting your existence first. Transitioning is, hands down, the best decision you will make for yourself.

Even though transitioning is a challenge in itself, and you will spend several years losing friends and family members and desperately searching for other trans people, you will be thankful every single day that you are still alive – and that you are alive as the man that you know you are. In the midst of struggles and heartbreak that come with life changes, keep in mind that one day, your family will use your correct name and pronouns, you will meet other trans people who will become lifelong friends, you will become involved in the community you always wanted, you will meet a man who teaches you what it means to truly love and be loved by someone, and you will begin to love and respect yourself for your identity, perseverance, and unapologetic advocacy for all members of the LGBTQ+ community in the South.

My parting words from a twenty-eight-year-old you to a ten-year-old me are...there is not a single thing wrong with you. Your heart is so beautiful, compassionate, and empathetic, and you deserve more than what you receive. You are a boy, a man, through and through, and one day, your body will reflect that. When you experience discouragement, rejection, and heartbreak, please remember that life has so much more to offer you and you will experience unconditional love and connection with the right people at the right time.

Keep your head up and know that, like Chaz Bono, you will one day walk confidently down the street and nothing anyone says will even come close to touching you. Life is full of good and bad, ups and downs, victories and losses, successes, and failures. But life is worth living, and please consider it a certainty that one day you will realize being trans is more beautiful, your existence is more beautiful, and life is more beautiful than you could ever imagine.

From,
A 28-Year-Old You
Kalvin Benfield

# TO THAT SWEET, TALENTED, CREATIVE, LOVING, AND BRAVE LITTLE BOY THAT STARTED MY JOURNEY IN LIFE,

Throughout your life, you knew you had the love and support of your mother once you were old enough to figure it out. She gave you the mindset and drive to be the child I just mentioned. With her love and encouragement, the sky was the limit!

Most of the kids in elementary school thought you were so cool because of your creative and artistic abilities. The ones that didn't you had to physically fight at times. When Junior high started, everything changed. A lot of the kids were new! The kids who went to school with you previously had changed their minds! You were not cool anymore, instead most were scared to hang with you. From then on, school was not easy, and you had only a few close friends.

They didn't know the secrets you were hiding since you were in the first grade. You felt like you were in the wrong body - that you were meant to be a girl. With everything going on at the time, your depression hit like a ton of bricks. You thought about ending your young life because the stress from being bullied was almost too much to take. When your new band partner took his life because of being bullied, it made you realize what heartbreak your mother and loved ones would endure.

Somehow through all of this, you managed to have so much strength! I can assure you now as an adult, when folks look or comment, It's mostly positive. You will go on to become a star in the LGBTQ community. You will be looked up to as a transgender female, entertainer, and activist. You will obtain accolades, crowns, and awards during your adult life. You will get to perform in many venues all over North Carolina and the surrounding states - even as far away as Hawaii!

You'll have many more family members to come on board with love and support. You will also work in public in two different yet exciting careers, make-up artistry and veterinary medicine. You also seize the chance to educate people about being transgender. You'll gain a ton of friends and fans. Life is a lot easier because of the growing strength you passed on to me. Setbacks will happen because that's just life! I'm strong because of you. I can get through it because of you!

When I look back, I say thank you to you - my little hero!!!

Jamie Monroe

A transgendered woman, entertainer, animal lover, activist...a human being.

# DEAR LITTLE ONE, REMEMBER HOW YOU GOT HERE,

When I was a little boy, I lived in East Meadow on Long Island. I was light and free. I talked all the time and to anyone.

I have always known that things weren't what they appeared to be and I wanted to know "why?"

The answers I got came back to me as words and questions. I didn't understand the words at first. What I did know was that when the words were spoken to me, I had better watch my step. I made sure I could get out of any situation I was in. And fast, before I could hear the words.

Girlie boy, fairy, pretty boy, and fageleh.

The boys at school and on my block questioned me.

"Why do you talk like a girl?"

"Why do you act like a girl?"

Worse than the words and the questions was the tidal wave I felt coming at me. Even before it washed over me, my neck would stiffen, and my stomach pound. The wave was so strong and powerful that it blurred the boys' faces, but I could feel them staring at me. When I felt most free and happy, out of my body and part of everything around me, right at that very moment, the wave hit and knocked me over. I never saw it coming.

The boys didn't like me. I wasn't like them. What I never understood was how I was different from them. It was in me, but I couldn't see it. There were no video cameras then and my family didn't have a tape recorder. The boys said I talked like a girl, but in my head, when I talked and heard my voice, it sounded just like theirs. In those circles of deep-voiced boys, in gym or Cub Scouts or waiting for the school bus, the world spun around, and I could feel the waves coming into shore to hit me. I knew it would be best for everyone if I disappeared.

I decided the best thing to do was to stop talking. I had already stopped looking anyone in the eye because that was when the words hit me. It was easy to live in my own world. No one screamed the words at me. No one told me they were going to beat me up.

I wasn't alone.

I was with the ladies.

I first met them on the television in my family's den. Our "set," as my father called it, was a black-and-white job, all that we could afford. At the bottom of the screen was a dull metal panel inscribed with the Magnavox logo, to its left were two brown and gray plastic dials. The set's constant yearning to be tuned in to one of its five channels forced one of us to get up off of the couch, walk over to it, and change the channel. When the channel dial broke off, my father showed us how to switch stations by using a pair of pliers to turn the metal rod inside the hole where the dial used to be.

My job was to move the rabbit ears Father had installed to aid our weak antenna. As he commanded me to move them "...to the left..." or "No, no, no....more to the right," I touched the wallpaper behind the set, its repeating pattern of houses and meadows made so hot from the set's glowing tubes that my fingertips felt the way the bottom of my feet did whenever I ran across the sand to escape the waves.

Later, my father bought a color television, saying, when I asked him why, "Now we can watch President Johnson's war in color."

Without saying why, Father moved the black and white set into my bedroom. That was when the ladies made themselves known to me. I discovered movies on "The Late Show," "The Late Late Show," and "The Million Dollar Movie." They started at 11:30 PM and played until dawn. The summer when the ladies came to me was very hot. At night, everyone in the neighborhood left their windows open. I turned the lawn sprinklers on at midnight and left them on for an hour or two to cool things down. In the middle of the night, it was so quiet I could hear a neighbor sneeze a few houses down. If I listened hard enough, I could hear the stop light change its colors at the intersection two blocks away.

I was sure the popping sound of the gravel being crushed under the tires of the occasional passing car would wake the neighborhood up. Everyone slept. Occasionally, a breeze would come by and, though it couldn't reach my bedroom window, I could see the mimosa tree branches dance outside the window. I lived in the night, the darkness, the quiet, and the solitude. There were no waves, no relentless tides. I laid on my bed in my underwear, the television positioned so that when I propped my head up on two pillows all I could see was the large black and white screen, as the blue light from the television reflected against the brown paneled walls of my bedroom.

I had already met the first two ladies in the den on the television series "Peyton Place." Gena Rowlands played Adrienne Van Leyden, old man Peyton's mistress, a woman whose treachery caused her husband to jump to his death from the balcony of their stylish high-rise. Lee Grant was Stella Chernack, a biochemist, whose tough heart had run from a murky past in Los Angeles.

The first time Lee was on the show, my mother said, "She's so wonderful. This is her first job since she was blacklisted."

My father laughed and said, "Roy Cohn wanted her to testify against her husband and now she's doing this crap?"

If somebody tried to manipulate Stella, she would have none of it. Her eyes narrowed as she straightened her back and brushed the hair off her face with a quick flick of her hand, as Stella gave her adversary a look that went right through him.

Late into the night, I discovered Lee Grant made her first movie, "Detective Story," in 1951, before she was blacklisted. And that Gena Rowlands played Rock Hudson's lover in one of her first movies, "The Spiral Road." Soon, Geraldine Page arrived in versions of Tennessee Williams plays. At last, Kim Stanley appeared in "The Goddess," which was repeated nightly for a week on "The Million Dollar Movie." I watched every showing.

I didn't understand it at first. I thought Kim was plain and awkward, but at the same time she was beautiful, she moved like a cat. Kim floated like the mimosa branches. Finally, I understood. Kim was imagining that she was beautiful, she believed that she was the character, a movie star goddess in Hollywood.

I made it through high school, staying up all night, watching the ladies as I sipped Pepsi with chipped ice, my cat Lady lying next to me, her all fours extended out in cat surrender. These women and others came out of the screen to me. I could feel the still air of the rooms they lived in, the stiff brocade of chairs they sat on, the sharp cut of the clothes they wore, and the tightness of the brake pedals their high-heeled shoes pushed against.

I did research. I sat in the library, whose soft Naugahyde couches made my skin feel the three AM lightness only Lady and I knew about. I read the plays and books the movies were based on. Sitting in partitioned booths, I ran spools of shiny microfiche, on which I discovered interviews with the ladies and the directors and writers of their movies. I had to know everything about what the night was showing me.

In the mornings, after I had watched movies until dawn, the boys played baseball or lacrosse on the street in front of my house.

I could no longer see or hear them.

#

Fifteen years later, I had been living in Hollywood for six months, trying to make it as a stand-up comic, when I got a job as a nurse at Cedars-Sinai. When my head nurse, Thordis Brandt, introduced herself to me, I knew who she really was, having immediately recognized her accent and hourglass figure.

"Weren't you the German bride in 'Funny Girl?'" I asked. Before Thordis could answer, I said, "And the other night, I saw you on the Z channel in 'Myra Breckinridge.' You were whipping John Houston on a massage table."

Calmly brushing her hair back like Stella Chernack, Thordis answered, "That was long ago...the sixties, darling. And always remember, this is Cedars and I'm Swedish."

Thordis had drawn blood from John Houston, I kept her secret. Besides, even though I was in the tribe, what if my patients found out that on the weekends, I was working at my first comedy gig, as the MC of a male strip show at a run-down bar, called the Dunes, on the beach in Venice? What if my patients knew that the nice Jewish punk who massaged their backs before bedtime was--as an homage to Adrienne Van Leyden, occasionally, and only occasionally, and without my encouraging finding fifty-dollar bills slipped into my satin shorts, an incentive for me to introduce a patron to a particular dancer?

One afternoon at Cedars, having listened to the tribulations of faded movie stars before administering their much-needed enemas, I found myself hanging out in the lobby on a break. Gena Rowlands walked out of the gift shop with a pack of Marlboro Reds and sat down next to me.

"Admiring the art?" Gena asked. While she pointed her cigarette at the Miro print in front of us, Gena's left hand slowly pushed her thick blonde hair off of her forehead.

I might have possibly been pretending to look at the Miro instead of Gena.

"Actually, I'm waiting to see which celebrities besides Faye Dunaway exit the AA meeting down the hall," I answered.

And then I lost it. Not because Gena was laughing at my joke, but because she was doing the Gena Rowlands thing with her hair. She always did it, before she told someone just how things were going to be. Or like in "Gloria," after she pumped a gangster full of bullets on a muggy New York City street in the quiet of an early summer afternoon. All I could do was babble away about how much I liked her in "Peyton Place."

"I died in 'Peyton?" Gena asked. "Odd what people remember. And yet, you have. What is it you do?" Gena's hair remained mysteriously in place, as we rhythmically blew smoke through our noses.

"I'm a comic," I said. "I've been trying to get an audition at the Groundlings for months, but they won't see me because I don't have any stage experience." Gena stood up to leave, did the hair thing again, and looked at me the way she looked at the gangster right before she plugged him.

"Tell them you were in the play John, and I did here. It will get you in and if you're funny enough, they won't care that you haven't been on the stage."

Her sunglasses lowered over her green eyes, the spikes of Gena's red silk pumps tapped softly against the polished brown ceramic tiles as she walked toward the lobby's South Tower, which was thankfully not the one hosting the star-packed AA meetings.

Two months later, my director at the Groundlings, Tim Stack, was once again arguing with me, as was his wont. Tim was always on me about something, stage left, stage right, stage directions, stage whispering, and some nonsense about cheating out.

"You've got to be the worst actor I've ever seen," Tim shrieked. "How were you ever in a John Cassavetes play?"

"John wasn't like you, Tim." I pushed my imaginary hair off my forehead and fixed my Stella Chernack stare on Tim.

"John didn't trip like you. He let my emotions dictate where I should be on stage. We didn't need to know where our marks were because we made our marks emotionally. He would've slapped me silly if I ever cheated on my performance. Why do you encourage that?"

I took acting classes. I learned to have the most intimate of conversations onstage while looking straight out into the audience and not into my fellow actor's eyes. What I never learned, what no one has ever asked me is: how could a boy who was so terrified of speaking out loud and being seen become a man who only feels safe when he is standing in front of people and talking.

That is the why I cannot answer.
Jake Epstine
Actor

# DECISIONS, DECISIONS, DECISIONS

L ooking back over my almost eighty years of life, I recall a time when personal frustration was at an all-time high and I had to make an important decision that would perhaps change my life completely for better or worse.

I was a high school teacher in rural Michigan at the time and enjoying a twelve-year career in a small but upscale community. It was the 1960s. I didn't make much money back in those days, but the gratification I received in preparing young adults for college and successful years beyond made up for the lack of income. At least it did for a while.

I had one very dark secret at that time, however, that hovered over my persona like a dark ominous cloud over a churning sea. Very few people, if any, knew the true me. I had thought for most of those twelve years that if I revealed myself to my community in any way, shape, or form, the dark cloud hovering above would eventually become a hurricane, and my life would be a sinking ship like the Titanic.

That's when it dawned on me that I could choose to live my life exactly the way I had been living it, or I could throw a monkey wrench into my boring existence and change things up - hopefully for the better. After much thought, I chose the latter.

I knew that for me to make a significant change in my life, it would have to include a new location geographically. I would have to resign from my teaching position in the school system and leave the small rural location where I resided somewhat happily and easily for the last twelve years. That, indeed, was a scary thought. I was thirty-four years old, practically middle-aged, crying out loud. And where was I proposing to go? I was clueless. I had no idea. The one thought I knew for sure was that I wanted to live in a big city where I could find a decent job, feel free, enjoy the social life, and thrive without guilt. But where might that be? One night after a few glasses of wine I wrote down on a sheet of paper twelve cities that appealed to my sense of discovery where I could find that pot of gold at the end of the rainbow. Those cities included the Big Apple (New York City), Miami, New Orleans, Chicago, Boston, Dallas, Houston, Austin, St. Louis, Kansas City, Seattle, Tacoma, San Francisco, and Los Angeles. On my third glass of wine, I decided to cover my eyes and drop my left index finger (left-handed, I am) to the list and I promised myself that wherever it landed I would land as well. Yikes, what was I getting myself into?

As it turned out, I would be moving to California, practically all the way across the country to the "City by the Bay." It couldn't have been a more perfect fit for rather obvious reasons if you have thus far read between the lines in this epistle.

The next decision to tackle was finding a place to live and then finding a rewarding job to commence an entirely new life. I only knew one person in San Francisco and luckily enough I was invited to inhabit an empty bedroom for as long as I needed it. Strangely enough, being the outgoing person that I am, one day I placed a sign on my jacket (it was damn cold in S.F.) that read that I was looking for an apartment in this "wonderful" neighborhood. Off to the market I went (where Julia Child used to shop – yes really) and sure enough, while at the checkout line, the woman behind me tapped me on the shoulder and told me about an apartment about two blocks away that just had placed a "For Rent" sign at the entry of the Edwardian twelve-unit building. My sign strategy worked as I ended up residing in that building for twenty-nine years.

Another big decision I had to make was how was I going to pay the rent on my new flat and feed myself after I ran out of dough. I made the move with a little monetary padding to keep me financially afloat for a while, but that wouldn't last long. I decided that in my search for employment instead of going off in a direction outside of my skill set, I would focus on my B.A. degree in English. I was a decent writer with a lot of teacher training, so that was the path I was going to follow. As it turned out, and as luck would have it, one day when I was searching the want ads, I came upon an ad for a secretarial position at a major brokerage firm in the financial district of the city. They wanted someone with strong language and writing skills.

Could I, should I, do I really want to be what was uniquely referred to as a male secretary? Oh, what the heck. I'll go ahead and try and set up an interview. Nothing ventured, nothing gained, I thought.

After I faxed my resume to the office, the response came back that I was way overqualified, but if I wanted to pursue the interview, they would see me later on that week. I went for it. When the day of the interview came, I tried my best to look sharp and be as enthusiastic and friendly, but professional, as possible. Very quickly I was given a written grammar and spelling test for evaluating my skill set and told as well at the time that no one had ever scored a perfect total. I think the test giver was quite astonished when she told me that I, indeed, had scored one hundred percent. There was one caveat, however, that I thought could make or break me with the interview. It was to point out that I had found a punctuation and grammatical error in the instruction section of the test that maybe should be corrected before other candidates take it. At that point, I debated with myself whether to remain quiet or point it out. Of course, I danced with the devil and pointed it out, and, low and behold, as a result of that decision I got the job. Always trust your gut, well, almost always!

I ended up working for that brokerage firm in San Francisco for twelve years and from my entry as a "male secretary" I eventually rose to a position as head of Human Resources for three hundred and fifty employees. And it was all because of finding an error that needed corrected!

Unfortunately, that job came to a conclusion when the firm moved our office to Denver, Colorado. I was given the opportunity to go there as well, but I chose to stay in San Francisco. Nope, it was on to a new chapter in my book of life and if I started over once, I could do it again. Little did I know that the new chapter would be my final chapter in my professional working career before I retired.

At this stage of my life, I knew that security in retirement would be my main goal and objective, so I tried to focus on employment possibilities that would bring California state pension benefits to my later years. I stuck with my talents and after many tries of finding a position with the University of California, San Francisco, (approximately fifteen applications), I finally was offered a temporary slot in their clerical pool. Do I accept it or keep my search going in another direction? I more than humbly accepted the position and in the fifteen years of working for UCSF, my final position there before I retired in 2006 was as Assistant to the C.I.O of the university, campus side. It was probably the most fulfilling and fun job that I experienced during the course of my entire working career.

And, yes, there is a moral to this story. After the lessons I have learned throughout my lifetime of education and employment, the simple truth of life can be stated in three words. "Trust your gut." Prepare your pathway, chart your course, maybe take some chances along the way, but always make yourself number one. If you slip up you can always recover in time. Never give up. Now that I look back at those early years, I can fully understand how important it is to keep your eyes, mind, and heart always open and moving forward. I might finally add that a little bit of luck along the way never hurts!

Jack Webster
Writer

# HEARTBEATS

It was a normal Memorial Day weekend of respecting those who gave their life to the Military. My father was at rest in Arlington National Cemetery after his thirty years as a Naval Aviator and advisor. But that was to quickly change as soon as we arrived home after dinner at the in-laws. My baby brother was sobbing so hard on the phone I could not understand him. He'd been given the task to call me and let me know that my older sister - by three hundred and sixty-four days - and her almost nineteen-year-old son had been killed in a car accident earlier that day by an underage unlicensed driver. I was just stunned.

We are a family of seven children and always will be, even with those we have lost. My younger self in 2001 didn't know anything about sudden loss and grief. I would have told my younger self to wrap my own arms around myself and cry. Instead, I was strong for my own family as I told them what had happened. I pushed away my sorrow and prepared for our daughter's high school graduation the next night. She was at the top of her class.

When I boarded the plane from California to Alabama the next day to be with my siblings and parents in Alabama, I would tell my young self - it's all right to show your emotions around strangers. I was so tired from holding it all in. My sorrow was so painful. I managed to keep myself strong through many years until my younger brother was killed by a drunk driver in 2011. Another sudden knife twist in my heart but by this time I was able to grieve openly and with purpose unlike in 2001. This was due to learning about grief in the interim and coming out to the light where you never stop missing your loved ones but wish them well in their afterlife.

It is a transformative feeling my younger self had no idea how to deal with, so I had many sad lost years prior to this. I will always love and remember those lost every day with dignity and occasionally tears which I now let freely run whether I am alone, in the grocery store, or simply looking back at lovely memories. Hearing certain music can bring them all back to me in a heartbeat and after all, isn't that where love lives?

Between the heartbeats, my younger self, is real love.

Jeanne Antos
Sister, mother

# DEAR SEVENTEEN-YEAR-OLD SELF,

Things are really hard for you right now. You have no idea how you're going to make it through all of it and hope seems to be in short supply. I can't lie to you—things are going to be hard for a long time. They will get better, and then get worse again, and then they'll be the best they've ever been. Just when you think you've gotten through all the worst pain you could feel, you'll find that life will humble you with something new that's horrible in a way you've never experienced.

That sounds bleak, doesn't it? I bet you thought that this letter was going to offer some hope and encouragement about the future, that everything will get better. Well, it does, and it doesn't. While life will continue to knock you around as life always will for each of us, you will still be growing and changing. Right now, you have very little control over your world, and you don't have the means to live your life the way that makes you feel safe, happy, and fulfilled. I think that's the hardest part of being a kid or teenager - the utter lack of control over your life. You can't just escape whatever is hurting you because you have to rely on adults to take care of you. Even in the best circumstances, that can be hard for a seventeen-year-old. And you are not in the best circumstances.

Your life as an adult is not going to look like you thought it would. You're not going to graduate from college at twenty-two and have your career started right after that. You're not going to meet the love of your life and have all your dreams come true in the next five years. You're not going to be a successful actor and get to travel the world before settling down in a beautiful Tudor-style home before you hit thirty. You're not going to lose seventy-five pounds and finally be able to feel comfortable in your body because of it. You're not going to have all the things you want to happen the way you want them.

You are not going to reach a single goal at the time that you think. You're only going to last six months of your first run in college because you're not ready - and that's okay. You'll be a better student because of your age. You're not going to graduate from college until you're thirty. You'll have the same crappy job for years while you work on figuring things out. Then you'll get into a job that sets you on the path you were always meant to be on. It will be the best and worst job you've ever had up to that point. You will learn more about the world and about yourself than you could learn anywhere else. That job will eventually lead you back to school and it allows you to support yourself until you graduate.

You're going to continue to have brief, failed relationships and scare people away for many years. There's going to be a lot of heartbreak and longing for love. You're going to make a lot of stupid decisions that hurt you and other people. You're going to keep repeating these patterns until you recognize them, and you start to heal. Then you're going to meet the love of your life- and even that won't look like how you think it's supposed to look. It's not a happy ending with the fireworks and the music, but a partnership with someone that you work at. And that's even better. When you find him and you fall in love, you'll see he was worth the wait and the heartache. Each year with him gets better as you grow together.

But there will be loss - a lot of it. More than the average person will experience at our age(s). You've just had your first big one. I'm sorry to tell you that you have a few more coming up and they are going to be incredibly difficult. But you are going to get through the losses and the love you have for the people in your life will only grow deeper. You're going to get closer to your family and watch it grow.

You're going to go to therapy, which will be huge for you. Eventually, everything we go through catches up with us. You're going to learn how to love yourself and how to require your brain not to be on guard all the time and worry non-stop. Well, it's going to get a lot better anyway. It's probably not going to go away completely. But that's okay too. You'll accept that you're a person with anxiety and you'll help others navigate it too.

You'll still have the same best friend in seventeen years, which I think is pretty cool. You'll have ups and downs with him too. You're actually going to stop talking for a year and it's going to be awful. But you'll work it out and your friendship will only get stronger. Over the years it will evolve just like the two of you. You'll form strong friendships with other people too. By now, you've learned that no one person can be everything to you and you're better for it.

You're going to change in a lot of ways but fundamentally remain the same. That sounds like it doesn't make sense. I could give you examples, but I don't want to give away all the surprises. One thing that doesn't change, and the thing I've always liked about us the most- you will continue to be who you are whether or not you are meeting other people's expectations. You're going to live your life however you want, like the things that you like, make the choices that you make, and be proud of all of it. You are not going to allow anyone to decide who you are supposed to be because of how you look, your gender, or where you are. What's different in the future is that you're not going to feel bad about it anymore. You're going to stop trying to please everyone. You will make no apologies for just being you. You will continue to grow, and you will flourish.

These next seventeen years are completely different from the first seventeen. While you might be looking back on your life now and wishing things had been different, you'll change your mind. Every embarrassment, every failure, every ounce of pain and fear and hopelessness - every moment led you to where we are now. I promise you - it will be magnificent.

Claudia Hooker
Therapist

# DEAR SARAH,

You need to know some things as you approach your sophomore year in high school. Things were rough in your middle school years, but they will prepare you for the future. And I don't mean building character. There will be some happy moments. We will start with the sour.

**Family**

This has been a turbulent time. Ever since your fifteenth birthday things drastically changed and you don't know which side is up. Not knowing who to trust terrifies you. Grandpa died and you watched who you thought were people that loved you turn their backs on you and lie.

As you dreamt about your visits with your grandfather, he warned you of whom to trust. To protect your dad at all costs. That you should never entrust your grandmother with anything ever again.

You will question Mom about this, and she will come clean. This will add to your worry. The sleepless nights. The pulling away from friends. All of this will be something you hide. You will spiral into a deep depression.

Tensions are high. You will find solace in the arts. Theatre, chorus, and travel will be your comfort.

**School**

You will experience your first taste of the stage as a freshman. Finally, a stage play comes your way sophomore year. While it's only five lines, you will have the bug and turn away from pursuing law.

Traveling to Niagara Falls and Canada is a highlight. Taking pictures will pay off and you will be published in the school literary magazine.

The love of history will never leave you.

Debating with Dad over dinner never gets old.

Sarah Daniel
Author

# DEAR SELF,

I wish I had some words of wisdom to share with you. Something I could tell you that would prove everything is going to be okay. That your future self-accomplished something amazing or that the world changed to be this incredible place. The truth is I can't tell you any of those things. Not because they didn't happen but because I wouldn't want you to change the past knowing what the future holds. Part of what made me who I am today is because of all the hardships I faced. The tribulations I had.

What I will tell you is all those times you were afraid to speak up, to stand out, to be true to yourself. All those times you were too afraid because of all the bullying you endured helped you become one of the strongest, most outspoken, kind, loving people I know. Although you also have a very hard exterior and you don't allow people in easily, when you do let people in, it's one of the most wonderful things to witness.

I will tell you that you will create a family that is so incredible and amazing your heart is overjoyed. All you want to do is take care of them and give them the best life you can.

Everything you expected life to be turned out to be better in some weird twist of events. I don't want you to change who you are now but know you will change as you age, and you grow. The world is going to change with you, but you are going to love your life and are going to love yourself.

Love Your Future Self,

Jillian Spain
Teacher & author – The Day the Pride Parade Came to Town, an upcoming children's book from Gold Dust Publishing.

# DEAR PAST REBEKAH,

I thought I would be writing to a child-version of myself, but I find myself more drawn to not so long ago. The year is 2018. Everything around you speaks to your success. You own and operate your own successful business. You've lived up and down the eastern coast working on projects you're passionate about. You've produced theatre, created roles through playwriting, brought those roles to life by finding and employing wonderful performers in four different cities across three different states, and even performed on national TV shows. You are under thirty years old and are the vision of success for so many…and you're drowning. You're a workaholic, the only time you consider for yourself is when you walk your dog. You're borderline alcoholic, your connection with your friends is strained, you're dating a covert abuser, and you're so, so tired. Do you know how I know this? Because everything I just mentioned are things I no longer struggle with. I had to first figure out what my issues were, hold them into the light, address them, and - most importantly - make applicable change.

I write to you from 2023. You moved out to your own place. You're in a different city. You're dating a woman. You learned how to distance yourself from your phone by limiting your notifications and only using social media for work. Speaking with people one-on-one and in small groups has become the priority. You travel all over the country to visit those who make you feel most like yourself without airs or requirements. You work fewer hours and get more done. You give yourself things to look forward to and you're your own boss. You even continue to provide employment to others whom you have grown to love, trust, and enjoy, who are spread out all over the country. Your dog has since passed and you honor her every time you take a walk by thanking her for all she did for you. She saw you when you needed to be seen most. As you, just as you are. Cherish all the time you have with her. Your biggest lesson to learn from her is that your worth is not based on what you can do for others. Your worth is based on what you can do for yourself and then what it is you choose to share for others.

You must wonder how you've been able to do all these things. You'd never believe me then, but here goes: You run a social media page based on your conversations with ghosts. Yep. You're a medium. I know what you're thinking, "I don't see them! I don't hear them! I don't see other's passed loved ones! There's no way!" You have plenty to learn. Passed loved ones are a specific frequency. You'll learn this frequency with others (though you've already been doing it for your own family), but more naturally, you've always been able to pick up on ghosts. Don't shake your head. You have. You just don't like to think about how many times you've been scared, and you had no understanding of just what you could do about it.

You started opening up to being able to perceive spirits when you moved to Wilmington, North Carolina. Yes, Wilmington. Seems random, doesn't it? Trust me, you have destiny here. You were not meant to be drawn in this direction until you were open to receive that destiny. You figured out your own language of perception that turned out to be just as valid as the mediums you had seen on TV.

First, you made videos about photos captured on the ghost tours you led. Eventually, all the theatres close up for a worldwide pandemic and the safest way for you to continue making content is to hang out with those who can't spread the sickness: ghosts. You'll see some of your darkest times when the theatre isn't available for you to throw yourself into. All the grief, concerns, worries that you ran from for years will catch up to you. But you stop running. You let them catch up. Then you allow yourself to properly and deeply heal. It's painful and so, so worth it.

Your following grows the largest when you begin to share stories of your conversations with ghosts. You started the series at random based on experiences you weren't fully believing you were having at the time. So many people reached out to you saying that they were feeling seen. Hundreds of thousands of people watched as you replayed the only theatrical outlet you had. You transformed what you had done on stage and screen into what you could do on your phone all while managing to make it autobiographical and genuine. So many people believed in you. They wanted to meet you. You started setting up times to meet the public.

Eventually - and much faster than you expected - you put yourself and your hard-earned talents of reading psychic energy out there. Within days you had sold out two months of meeting times. When five months sold out, you quit your other jobs to keep up. On and off, your bookings sold out between six and twelve months in advance. People often have their bookings with you and immediately book again. You have a Patreon with amazing and kind people who fund your film scheduling. Most importantly, you have time off to breathe. By putting yourself out there and sharing your growth, struggles, healing, and pain on a public platform, people connect with you and are inspired by you.

Life is funny. You'll learn how to laugh. You'll learn that how you see the world is a strength and that many others feel seen by what you share about yourself. You learn how to say no. You also learn how to say yes to yourself. You learn to take care of yourself and believe me, that is a priceless skill. So often people will want to know how it is that you do what you do. Each time you tell them that you are here today because you put your mental health and self-awareness first. Those who truly see you and respect you will honor that and work on it for themselves.

Your entire world will change in a very short amount of time. And you're going to be so much better for it. Keep your old friends close even though you're all spread out across the country. Keep in touch with your mom. She supports you no matter what. Be open with her and your found family. And please, when you get a bad or uncomfortable feeling about someone, believe in yourself. There will be those who come into your life who want what you have but are not putting in the work that you've been putting into yourself. You are not a holding place for other people's jealousy and cruelty. Sometimes you will be an ice-breaking ship navigating other's unhappiness. Other times you will be a sailboat that drifts effortlessly in just the right amount of wind. Allow yourself to be drawn to those who build you up. They will be the ones who help to carry you through when you need it most.

Have you been wondering how you wound up with a girlfriend? Don't. You'll leave so many "closets" in such a short amount of time. While it is understandable you will want to be tentative, please know that when you make positive moves for yourself that those who truly care about you will be the most excited...and likely not even surprised. I wish I could say that being on the other side of it makes things so much easier. Yes and no. The same issues persist only when you stop applying what you've learned from the past. The good news is you are having to repeat mistakes less and less. Give yourself grace. You're worth it. I know you don't believe me right now, but you're worth all of it. Worth being loved. Worth loving yourself. If there is one last piece of advice I could give, it would be to learn to say this to yourself: For all the love, care, and consideration I give to others, I am worthy of giving more and receiving more for myself.

I love you even when you don't always love you. You brought me here. I am grateful you made it.

Love,
Rebekah Carmichael
Rebekah The Ghost Guide
Spiritual Consult & Mediumship

# MY DARLING,
# DEAREST ME,

Y ou are enough.

I know it doesn't seem like it. I know things are tough. You're out of step with the world around you. You're lonely. You're desperate for someone to love you as you are. You're exhausted from pretending that others' opinions don't matter. You just want to fit in somewhere.

I'm here to tell you that you will. One day not too far from now, you're going to find your place, your people, and the true love that you so desperately crave. I won't lie, though. There's going to be a lot of heartbreak along the way. You're going to make and lose friends, find and lose love, and your world is going to open up into its most glorious, beautiful version of itself.

And it is not at all how you imagine it's going to be.

Right this minute, you're an awkward, young teenager sitting in the library during lunch. You don't have many friends, and the ones you do have are either not at school today, or they're off doing things with other people. You're reading a book—Frankenstein, strangely enough—and sympathizing with the creature. Even though you weren't created in the same manner, the pain of abandonment resonates within you. You know, even this early in life, that you're different. You're not like those around you. But right now, you have no idea what that means.

But you will. You're going to transcend this little, incestuous pile of pubescent waste, move above and beyond what the parameters of your life would suggest. Your small-school-small-community nightmare won't last forever.

I'd tell you not to be afraid of what's to come, but that would be doing you a disservice. You need fear, and you need the experience. In the next few months, you're going to have your first real experience with death. It's going to make you question religion, and that struggle will last for years. You'll figure it out, though.

You're also going to experience betrayal. That one is really going to suck.

You're going to lose touch with a good friend, but the two of you will reconnect once you're both in a better place. You're right to worry about her, but in the end, you're both going to be okay.

You're going to overcome your anxiety, too. Keep on top of your academics. Continue with the public speaking and debate activities. Those are skills you're actually going to use in the future. You can forget AP Physics and Calculus when you get to them though. You're going to ace the exams, but you're never going to need that shit again.

But that's all stuff that will come later.

At this very moment, all you need to do is keep reading your books. Keep listening to your music. Keep developing your sense of justice and don't ever let anyone tell you that your thoughts and feelings don't matter, because they do. One day you're going to be the one with the platform, able to use your words to empower others the way you never had. You just have to hold onto your courage and take the leap. In many ways, I still haven't fully built that platform, but I promise you, I'm going to get there. I'm doing it for both of us. So please, don't give up on yourself no matter how hard things get. Once you're me, you're going to remember those struggles. What you've yet to experience will shape me into the person I am today. It's not going to be easy, but I appreciate everything you're going to face for my sake.

Though…if I may, allow me to spill a few secrets early for you.

1. That silent desire for people to accept you isn't necessary. People already *do* accept you. And they will continue to accept you. You're a pretty amazing kid, even if you can't see it. You become a pretty awesome grown-up, if I do say so myself.

2. You do not have to define yourself by others' opinions and beliefs. Love isn't black and white, and it isn't binary. You aren't limited to loving one specific type of person, and you aren't limited to loving in one specific way. The sooner

you learn that it's okay, even for you, to love who you want to love without reservation and restraint, the better off you'll be. Love as fiercely now as you will learn to love in the future.

3. In a few years, you're going to meet someone that will turn your world upside down. Her presence will be brief and intense, and it will change every single fiber of your character. Though her exit will be one of the most painful heartbreaks of your life, she will be the one to force you onto the path that determines the rest of your life.

4. Learn to stand up for yourself. Just because you're an introvert doesn't mean you don't have the right to personal autonomy. You don't have to allow yourself to be bullied anymore. You'll continue to carry the scars you've already received for the rest of your life, but you don't have to let them define you. Let them be a source of strength for your character.

5. It's okay to not be okay. It sounds cliché, but it's true. It's perfectly okay to falter, but the one thing you must remember, above all else, is that when you fall…you get back up. Now get up.

There's still a whole lot more I haven't said. But you know what? You're just going to have to wonder about it. Above all else, though…remember that you're going to be okay. And no matter what, I'm proud of you.

See you in a few years, me. I love you.

S. H. Roddey
Author and cover designer

# HEY YOU,

Yeah, I can see you, hiding behind the boxes in the storage closet of the library. It's okay. You can come out.

Hey. It's going to be okay. No, I mean it. It is. I'm not going to tell the librarian. Or the other kids.

Come on out, okay? It's just you and me here right now.

Hey. Here's some ice for that bruise. Can I see your notebook? No, I'm not going to take it. It's okay. I'm not going to tell anybody.

Oh, yeah, this notebook. The notebook where you write down all the rules about what makes people mad and what gets you in trouble. Yeah. You write a lot in this.

How do I know? Because I'm you, and I used to write in this.

No, seriously. I'm you, twenty years ahead. Swear. Just like Charles de Lint wrote, yeah? Time can move around like water in a pool. You read the books; you know this.

Okay, breathe. Just breathe.

Okay. Let me tell you something. No, not lottery numbers; this doesn't work that way. But I can tell you about life. About how it's going to be.

Truth is, you're probably always going to want to find somewhere quiet and safe to hide sometimes. There are always going to be bad days. But one day that place you go will be a private space lined in soft blankets and pillows, not a closet the librarian forgets to lock. You'll have this room where only you ever go because the person you live with knows you need a safe place. And outside that door, you'll have a warm, safe house where nobody screams, and nobody cries at night. You'll have your own room full of books. It will be quiet. It will be gentle. I know it doesn't help now, but it is going to happen.

I know there's not a lot of safe places right now. I know there's a lot of fear, anger, and screaming at home. I know there are so many cousins that there's never a second of peace, and there's always somebody telling you to stand up straight or go do a chore or fix your hair. I remember. I know the kids at school are jerks. I remember the words and the fights. I know some days it feels like the only thing you can do is curl up and wait for everything to stop.

I know.

But I swear it won't be like that forever.

One day you're going to meet a great girl who loves you, and she'll help you make things better. And then you're going to meet a great guy who sings with you all night and you'll fall for each other. He'll help you build a kind, quiet life.

I know it doesn't feel like it right now. But things are going to get better. You are going to get better. And one day, you'll be where I am saying it.

So, here's some stuff to add to your notebook.

- When you get your first job, look at the people who've been there for five years or more. If they look like they hate the job, get out of there.
- When somebody says something cruel to you, it isn't about you. It's about them.
- Sometimes people are going to be in pain. It isn't your job to fix every sign of unhappiness. Sometimes, all you need to do is sit there and be with them.
- People can yell at you when you're grown up. They can say mean things. But if they hit you, they go to jail. Keep telling yourself that when bosses or people in Target yell at you. Don't step back and don't flinch. The cost of actually touching you is really high, and even crazy jerks mostly know that. Let them shout and stand your ground.
- When you think you're beaten, just breathe. Even when it feels like there's nothing in the future. Just breathe. Every time you do, a little more of the future will open up.
- Be patient. Good work takes years to show. One day you'll look up, and tons of people will be talking about you like a success.

- Be kind. People in your family taught you to hurt somebody else when you're hurting. Don't do that. Ever.

Now, here's the big thing: what the family tells you? I know you can't ignore it. But it isn't as important as you think right now.

No. Seriously. Right now, it feels like the way the world is, because they're the only ones you hear from. They and the teachers at school aren't a lot better. When the only thing you ever hear is that you're klutzy, you're ungrateful, you're strange and awkward, and not very good at making decisions, yeah of course you think that. But that isn't the whole story. You know what you can do about changing the story?

Read. Read tons of books. Read everything you can get your hands on. I know you know some of this because you hide in the library. But try reaching beyond the folklore shelves. There's more out there. Here are some authors.

- Charles DeLint
- Anne Block
- Terry Pratchett
- Diane Duane
- Saundra Mitchell
- C.B. Lee
- Ray Bradbury
- Catherynne Valente
- Robin Wall Kimmerer

You'll find out you're not as weird as you think you are. And more than that, it's okay to be weird. It's okay to like the way boys smile, and the way girls turn their wrists and move their heads. You'll find out that it's okay to mess up. It's okay to make mistakes. It's okay to want to leave home and be somebody who isn't who your family wants you to be. I know they told you that you were born to be a part of the family. Born to always be on hand, to always help family, and to be there for your older relatives. I know they told you that the thing you're supposed to do is have kids to continue the family and take care of the elders.

That's why I'm saying you should read. Because the books will show you so, so many other futures you can choose. Will it all be fun? Oh, hell no. But it will be your choice. Not your mom's. Not your grandma's. YOURS.

Is it going to be hard? Yeah, sometimes. Is the family going to be mad? Oh yeah, Mom and aunties and uncles and even some cousins from all over the family are going to call and scream at you sometimes. But you know what? One day you just won't be bothered anymore. I mean, you'll be pissed off, yeah. Especially when they call you in the middle of a movie. Or at work. Here's a tip, don't answer. When they complain, stress that hard work ethic they always pitch at you. And one day, when they scream, it won't hurt the way it does now. They won't get to make the choices about what you should do anymore. You will. And because you're making the decisions for yourself, all their screaming won't be able to do anything to you. They won't be able to cold-shoulder you for days anymore because you'll be living states away. They won't be able to scare you because they'll just be a voice on the other end of a phone line. They won't be the only people who matter anymore. You're going to have good friends, and you're going to have acquaintances, and goals that you picked out for yourself. You're going to have someone special. The family won't be the only thing in your life.

And another thing. When you look in the mirror, don't think about what they say about you.

- There is nothing wrong with the way you look.
- Your skin is fine. There's nothing wrong with the color of your skin.
- You're not too big.
- You're not gawky.
- Your hair is not bad or unruly or a problem
- You're not unsophisticated.
- You don't like girls because it's easier than liking guys who aren't attracted to you, you hear me?
- You're not unattractive. You hear me?
- I'm going to repeat this. There. Is. Nothing. Wrong. With. The. Way. You. Look.

And as for having kids? The family doesn't get to tell you what to do with your body. For that matter, they don't get to tell you what you do with your time either. There will come a point when you get sick of letting them make you cancel plans or skip class to pick up grandma's groceries and deliver uncle's pills, and you'll say no. Most important of all, there will come a day when you realize it isn't your job to fix their pain and their sorrow. It never was. They told you it was, but that's because they got hurt a long time ago and they've been hurting each other ever since. You didn't do that. You don't have to fix it. And you don't even have to put up with it. You'll put your notebook full of rules down one day and walk away. And life really will go on after that. It'll get better. Don't forget that, okay?

Just hang on. Keep breathing. Even on the worst days, hang on. It'll be worth it. I swear.

I love you, Little Otter.

Liv

Olivia Wylie
Author & business owner

# A LETTER TO MY YOUNGER SELVES...

John, you are exactly who you were intended to be.
You are strong. You are courageous.
It will take many years for you to believe you are strong and courageous.

Your life is going to be incredibly complex because of who you are and who you find attractive. Do you remember the nine-year-old neighbor boy who let you touch his stomach when you were only four years old? That was a long time ago, the same year as the Stonewall riots. The physical contact wasn't because he demanded it. No, it was because you were very curious, and you were attracted in some kind of childish way. Those attractions to boys will change into attractions to men and will never go away. No matter how hard you pray, how long you fast, or how much therapy you receive, the attractions will remain.

You are exactly who you were intended to be.

As a developing child, you will be unapologetic in what brings you joy. You will wear saddle shoes, decorate cakes, twirl the baton, play the piano, and freely dance while hearing the applause of imaginary audiences. Your real audiences of family and a judgmental society will feel embarrassed because of you. You won't see the problem until sometime in junior high. The years when circles of peers are cruel and unforgiving. Your given name will be replaced by bullies who will call you Betty Crocker and Joanie. You will feel a lot of pain.

You will find your strength.

Although you have never voiced your attractions or even made sense of it for yourself, you believe there is no one near you who experiences anything similar or who will accept your differences. Through asides in church, school, and family gatherings you are fully aware your loving family and greater society don't want you to be gay. Sadly, you will listen to them hiding your desires and modifying your feminine expressions into feigned masculinity.

It's during junior high you find how to ward off the ridicule by hiding your passions and attractions. You become an athlete - a swimmer and a runner. All individual sports where you don't have to be in close physical contact with other boys because... you know... that contact seems to add to the internal torment that has been labeled as sin.

You will deeply hate that part of yourself.

This is during the 1970s when you see the news footage of "The Gays" and "Queers" in Greenwich Village and San Francisco. They wore short shorts, muscle shirts, leather caps, and boas. Believing if you acknowledge your gay orientation you would morph into one of the extreme examples on television. You will deeply hate them and any part of yourself resembling "Those Gays".

You will date many girls and women stuffing your attractions and desires away into the private hell becomes a way of life. Seen and Unseen, Darkness and Light. You will live in a vicarious dichotomy… an impossible balance.

But you will find your strength.

Your family and church will have you believe that same-sex attractions are wrong and sinful, something to conquer. You won't be able to sift through the church teachings and the redirection of coaches, teachers, and pastors for quite some time. Probably until your mid-thirties. There will be a lot of life to live and a lot of struggles before then.

You will find your strength.

Stuffing your attractions and desires away into the private hell becomes a way of life. You live in that dichotomy, the impossible balance for years. For the public to see, you become a pastor, date beautiful women, and accept the invitation for those dreaded blind dates with your parishioners' granddaughters.

Your dark nights become longer than your public days as you seek anonymous sexual intimacy from men in unhealthy encounters. The AIDS epidemic terrifies you from engaging in most risky sexual contact, but your drive creates you to be a sexual pariah and a liar.

You hurt people back then.

A word of advice... Try not to intentionally hurt people along the way.

You are discovered, found out on one of those dark nights. The Christian organization you were working with hooks you up with a faith-based counselor who also happens to be a minister. He is incredibly charismatic. Enthralled by his charisma and enticed by his attention, he will be a dear mentor. He and his family adopt you as their own. Sadly, his counsel holds that you are gay and that it is sin.

One day, you will find your strength.

The dichotomy grows and your internal torment will rage. Working to quell that rage and in your mentor's footsteps, you pursue ministry. In all appearances, you thrive while the dark night rages.

Eventually, your mentor sits with you in deep conversation and outs himself as a gay man... it will take your breath away and shatter all you thought to be true. You will not know how to handle the information and you will watch that dear mentor struggle sometimes worse than you. You had so much hope in him which will cause deeper pain and confusion.

Nothing will prepare you for that Thanksgiving week when you are thirty-two years old. Your mentor calls you in despair reaching out to say goodbye. He describes how he is being investigated for his sexual orientation and expression. He is not well and that night he will kill himself.

You will find your strength.

At his funeral, you see his body in the casket and know you must find a different path. One that allows you to love yourself in truth and congruence. You will need to figure something out because you see yourself lying there.

This is the first step to healing those dark nights. You are finding your strength. You work to shed the lessons learned and find your own truth.

You will find a therapist after sitting with five others. She doesn't encourage you to be gay or not to be gay. She sits with you in developing your own understanding.

This is the time when you start to soar.

A congruent and self-accepting life does not come freely. You have strength and must remain strong and courageous. Because the world still does not fully understand or accept you and will try to hurt you. You will be the victim of a hate crime with a gun pulled. You will lose jobs because of who you are, and you will be refused jobs. You still hear the scoff of junior high children from time to time.

Learning you are exactly who you need to be and become. Honest, congruent, authentic, and complete in so many ways.

You will stand in front of audiences, legislators, board members, and churches revealing your true self in support of others. They listen and hopefully, they hear the message you bring of your journey.

Life does seem to make sense now. You will get here where you find happiness within yourself. You will learn to accept yourself in fullness, both strengths and weaknesses. You will get here where you find yourself in a twenty-three-year relationship with the love of your life... a man. Your family will express their love for you and support you. Your career will soar. You will find mentors who come without their agenda but desire to see you flourish. They rejoice when you fly.

You are strong and courageous.

The people who matter will see that. They will see you, your empathy, your care, your resilience. Surround yourself with them.

You are strong and courageous.

John C. Nance, PhD, LCMHC-S, NCC, ACS
UNC Charlotte - Assistant Clinical Professor & owner of Behavioral Health Integrative Solutions where he specializes in working with adult survivors of early childhood trauma and catastrophic torture. As a TEDx speaker, John works to help develop anti-racist and anti-bigot ideologies. 704.287.4855

"History isn't something you look back at and say it was inevitable. It happens because people make decisions that are sometimes very impulsive and of the moment, but those moments are cumulative realities."

— Marsha P. Johnson

"Learn from the bad, build on the good. Let's make the world a better place by learning from and about our past."

– Jason M. Roach

If one or more of these letters hit too close to home (either personal harm or someone is doing harm to you) and you would like to talk to someone, these LGBTQIA+ national hotline numbers will have someone available to help. Please know that you are not alone, and you can get through this. We love you.

**Lesbian, Gay, Bisexual, and Transgender (LGBT) National Hotline:**
1-888-843-4564

**LGBT National Coming Out Support Hotline:**
1-888-688-5428
(1-888-OUT-LGBT)

**LGBT National Youth Talkline:**
1-800-246-7743
(1-800-246-PRIDE)

**LGBT National Senior Hotline:**
1-888-234-7243

**The Trevor Project**
Text START to 678-678 or call 1-866-488-7386

**Trans Hotline**
Call 1-877-565-8860 to reach the Trans Hotline 24/7.

**National Suicide and Crisis Lifeline**

Call or text 988 to get crisis/suicide support. Available 24/7

**Crisis Text Line**
Text HOME to 741741 in the United States to access free, 24/7, confidential text message crisis support.

**Teen Line**
Call 800-852-8336 Nationwide (6 PM - 10 PM PST) or text TEEN to 839863 (6 PM - 9 PM PST)

**National Sexual Assault Hotline**
Call 800-656-HOPE (4673) to chat with a trained staff member from a sexual assault service provider in your area. Available 24/7 and is confidential.

**Domestic violence, sexual assault, and sex trafficking**
Call (916) 920-2952 to get 24/7 support and information from WEAVE, for survivors of sexual assault, domestic violence, and sex trafficking.

**Substance Abuse and Mental Health Services Administration (SAMHSA) Helpline**
Call 1-800-662-HELP (4357) to reach SAMHSA's National Helpline, which is a confidential, free, 24/7 information service, in English and Spanish, for individuals and family members facing mental and/or substance use disorders.

**National Suicide Loss Helpline**
Call 1-800-646-7322 to get 24/7 support if you are grieving a suicide death.

**National Runaway Safeline**
Call 1-800-RUNAWAY (1-800-786-2929), to access support as a runaway youth. All services are free and 100% confidential.

# ABOUT GOLD DUST PUBLISHING

Gold Dust is working to provide an avenue and safe place for LGBTQIA+ and allied authors to share their artistic talents through fiction or non-fiction writings with the world. Our non-fiction side works to help preserve our LGBTQIA+ history in a world where books are constantly being banned. Our fiction side of the company provides entertaining tales for all ages featuring LGBTQIA+ characters or written by LGBTQIA+ authors.

Anyone, regardless of identity, may submit pieces. We accept submissions from allies and other non-LGBTQIA-identifying people. We do not accept pieces that are inherently homophobic or directly act against our missions. Fictional manuscripts depicting rape, incest, and other extreme material as romantic, or titillation devices will be automatically rejected. We will, also, not publish any content depicting graphic sexual content between minors.

For more information, please visit
www.golddustpublishing.com.

# ALSO AVAILABLE FROM GOLD DUST PUBLISHING

- The House on Dead Man's Curve – Jason Roach
  Available in eBook, Paperback,
  Hardback, & Audio

- Until Death – An Eric Kent Investigation: Case 1
  Available in eBook & Paperback

# Thank Yous

Gold Dust Publishing would like to issue a huge thank you to everyone who contributed, provided insight and advice, and helped gather submissions. We all worked together to make it happen.

Also, a huge shout out and thank you to our cover designer, Susan. She's been my rock through this entire project, and I greatly appreciate her.